PRAISE FOR

PAIN TO PEACE: SETTING THE SONGBIRD FREE

"Heartfelt and honest, like sitting down with a long lost friend. *Pain To Peace* is written like a beautiful stream of parables, designed to connect with the author's life story while helping you deeply reflect on your own life, so you can let go of what no longer serves you."

> *Dr. Jen Faber*
> Author of *"90 Day Life"*
> Transformation Coach & Mountaineer

"Dr. Mindi takes us on her own life's journey - starting as just a little girl - packed with fun and laughter along with sadness and pain. Her ginormous heart emotionally shares these very personal stories - the transforming moments of her life - along with the Scripture the Lord used to comfort her and give her wisdom for growth. Then come the heart-revealing questions for our own hearts to ponder. Be prepared to easily become immersed and intertwined in Dr. Mindi's path so that your own journey unfolds!"

> *Beverly Gillespie*
> Small Business owner

"As a fellow sojourner in ministry, motherhood, and as a health professional, I appreciate Dr. Mindi's ability to always remain authentic and approachable both personally and professionally. She has a unique way of engaging the masses and providing care for the "least of these." Being able to witness part of her journey in finding and exploring new freedom is humbling and inspiring. Keep flying my sweet soul sister, we are with you."

> *Kerin Cornett*
> Counselor
> Ministry Leader

Pain to Peace
Setting The Songbird Free

MINDI MILLER-JENTES, DC

A BLACK EYED SUSAN MEDIA PUBLICATION

Black Eyed Susan Media

Pain to Peace: Setting the Songbird Free
Copyright 2024 by Mindi Miller-Jentes, DC

This title is also available as a Kindle e-book. Visit www.amazon.com.

Requests for information should be addressed to:
info@BlackEyedSusanMedia.com

Library of Congress Cataloging-in-Publishing Data

Miller-Jentes, DC, Mindi, 1973-
    Pain to Peace: Setting the Songbird Free/ Mindi Miller-Jentes, DC.
    Includes bibliographical references.
    ISBN: 979-8-9898897-0-9   E-book ISBN: 979-8-9898897-1-6
    1.   Self-Help Techniques.   2.   Spirituality

Cover design & artwork by Proverbs Photography
Cover copyright 2024 by Black Eyed Susan Media
Printed in the United States of America

Black Eyed Susan Media coordinates speaking events for Mindi Miller-Jentes, DC.

For booking information:
www.BlackEyedSusanMedia.com
or call (562) 888-3718

To my husband, Mike,
for always loving me like Jesus loves His Bride.

To my children, Kayla, Korey, Kevin, and Katja,
may you always remember "It's not about you. It's
about what God does through you."

To Dr. Jen, thank you for pushing me to break out of
the cage of pain so I could find my peace. I shattered it!

To Martha, thank you for loving me and praying for
me all these years. I couldn't have done this without
your love and support.

To Nat, thank you for encouraging me to write a book
about "anything." I finally did it!

CONTENTS

INTRODUCTION

If you know me, you know I like to talk—like a lot. So, you would think it only seems natural for me to write a book. I could surely fill many pages. I can assure you, this was not natural. This book has been brewing for nearly 15 years. I've always wanted to write but never thought I had anything to say that people wanted to hear. That is the problem with being told you talk too much. You begin to believe what you have to say is not valued.

Several years ago, a friend made a point to tell me I needed to write a book. My reaction was one of shock as I asked, "About what?" He replied, "Anything! You're a really good writer." WOW! That was surprising to hear. So, in good humor, this book is all his fault.

It still took another four years of struggling over whether I had anything to say of importance, wrestling with how to structure the book, which genre, who would be my audience—you get the idea. I finally decided I would take my friend's advice literally. So, here we are today—a book about anything.

My name is Dr. Mindi Miller-Jentes. I'm a Christ follower, a former police officer's daughter turned pastor's kid, a pastor's wife, a mom, a grandma, a Harley chick, an Opera singer, a published Watercolor Artist, a Doctor of Chiropractic, a public speaker and now a published author. Born and raised mostly in the South, having also lived all over the East and West coasts, the Midwest, as well as Germany; I've lived a colorful life for the ripe young age of 50. The funny thing is none of that defines me. It just describes my roles, what I like to do, and where I've lived—which is a lot, I suppose.

To really know who I am would take the rest of these pages to fill. So, for now, let's just say I'm a passionate Jesus follower whose mission is to help people break free from their chains of pain, so they can finally find peace and live a life they have only ever dreamed about.

I chose many years ago to live my life in such a way that I refused to live in fear. Since I was a child, my favorite Bible verse was *"Haven't I commanded you to be strong and courageous? Don't be afraid or discouraged, for the Lord your God is with you everywhere you go"* - Joshua 1:9. That verse has made me a force to be reckoned with.

I am not afraid to take risks. I am not afraid to fail. I love deeply and probably too much. I am incredibly sensitive and emotional, yet strong as a rock and determined as a bull. Some would call that wild or dramatic—just like any good dramatic soprano should be! I'm resourceful, creative, spontaneous, and full of energy. Most of all, I think most of my friends would describe me as fearless.

I have accomplished many of my dreams, but I keep adding to my list. If the Lord allows me, I will accomplish those dreams too. My husband calls me "Dr. Bad Ass." He knows full well, that when I set my mind to something, it's gettin' done and there ain't nothin' stoppin' me!

Some people like all the energy about me. Yet some do not. I realize I am not everyone's cup of tea, but I am some people's shot of whiskey! So, whether you are a tea sipper or a whiskey shooter, I think you will enjoy this book about anything—though it is really about a life's journey towards liberation.

This book is written for anyone to read. You do not have to be religious to enjoy it. Just like I would not expect you to leave out parts of who you are, I cannot write freely without fully embracing who I am. So, you will find lots of Jesus-talk in here. I do not apologize for that. One thing you will also discover in the pages of this book, I also push against religious and cultural norms and traditions. If you recall, so did Jesus. No matter where you are in your faith journey, I hope you will find what I have to say inspiring.

Through some of my life stories, morning musings, and time spent listening for and experiencing the power of the Great Spirit; I hope you will find this book to ruffle your feathers, awaken your soul, inspire you to become more and more the person you were created to be. My goal is to see you chase after your dreams with renewed passion.

So, grab your drink of choice, sit back, and get ready to walk a few miles in my shoes as you find the motivation to DREAM BIG! After all, living in fear is not living. It is paralyzing.

It is time to get busy living the life you desire and deserve!

Singing I go...   ~Dr. Mindi

HOW TO USE THIS BOOK

This book is designed to allow you to read it in any order you prefer. Each chapter is self-contained, so you don't have to read it like a story. However, it is recommended that you read it from front to back at least once, so you can get a better sense of the overall direction of the book.

To help you reflect on the contents of each chapter, there is a dedicated section included at the end. This section has a set of questions and exercises for you to work through. Additionally, there is an extra blank page provided where you can jot down your thoughts, doodle, or even paint if you prefer.

In the following pages, I have outlined practical steps that you can take to help you overcome the pain that has shaped your life's journey. Each person's pain is unique and can be more or less traumatic than others. This book is not meant to address any specific pain, as each person's pain is their own. Comparing pain is unhelpful and can keep you trapped in your pain. Instead, it is more beneficial to focus on breaking free from the pain so that you can experience the peace you deserve.

PRECIOUS MEMORIES

"Precious memories, how they linger;
how they ever flood my soul."

—John B.F Wright, 1925

I will never forget one of the early churches my dad pastored. It was a good-sized church in a small borough in a valley of the Allegheny Mountains of Pennsylvania. For some reason, I remember a lot about that church building. It was a very large, red brick building with a white church steeple and bell tower in the center of downtown. The front doors opened to the sidewalk on W. Main St. The church is still there today, ministering to the needs of its community.

I remember what felt like a labyrinth of hallways and doors to enter and exit the building. One could get lost in that three-story building. I know I sure did as a child.

I remember the chrome coat racks mounted along the walls next to the foyers holding all the Sunday best winter coats. I remember umbrellas and hats with rain or snow boots lined up underneath on rubber mats to collect the water. I remember the soft touch of the fur-lined sleeves of the velvety soft women's coats and the rough scratchy feel of the men's wool coats, hoping that maybe someday when I got older, I too could wrap myself in such a pretty accessory to wear to church.

I remember slipping and sliding on the ice going to and from the big church parking lot and getting scolded for going outside to play in our good church clothes before my parents were ready to leave after service.

I remember the smell of the potent lemon cookie air freshener in the nursery and bathrooms. I thought, who eats cookies in a bathroom or the baby changing station of a nursery? Flowers would have been a more appropriate air freshener. What did I know? I was just a kid.

I remember the church building also had loudspeakers broadcasting the morning worship and preaching into the hallways, foyers, parlor, nursery, and bathrooms, so those throughout the building would not miss anything.

I remember the large oak-stained wall rack with white-trimmed black lettering that displayed weekly updates of Sunday morning, Sunday evening, Wednesday night, and Sunday School attendance, as well as weekly and yearly offerings.

I remember the big oak door off the main foyer that opened to the pastor's parsonage, though we never dared go near it. We didn't live there. My dad's predecessor, who had retired, still lived there with his wife.

I remember helping to fold the weekly bulletins at the welcome station in the main foyer. Each Sunday bulletin had a different picturesque scene on the front that coincided with the current season.

I remember the industrial avocado green carpet throughout, and the pretty oak-stained pews lined up so regally. I remember that the oversized pulpit, large communion table, and altar, as well as the trim surrounding the walls of windows on each side of the sanctuary all matched so beautifully.

I remember the funeral parlor in the church where grieving families would gather to mourn. The parlor had two large double oak doors with a long skinny window in each door on one side of the room and a coordinating avocado green, accordion-style wall partition that would open the parlor to the sanctuary on the opposite side of the room. On occasion after service, I would sneak into the parlor to play the old upright piano and sing hymns.

I remember there was a lady in our church who wore the coolest slide-on dress sandals with a cork wedge heel and a faux leather white bow tied across the toes. She wore these with nylons, as was common back in those days. I remember telling her that when I grew up, I wanted a pair of shoes just like hers. Note: That was a dream that thankfully, did not come true.

I remember my parents recalling time and again when I was just a baby before I could even talk, holding the bulletin like it were a songbook and singing at the top of my lungs all the way home from church.

I even remember the first time I sang a solo in church. I do not remember what song it was, but I remember that my dad sat on the front pew, crying while I sang. He still cries whenever he gets to hear me sing.

I remember one Sunday, an older lady was greeting my dad after his sermon. She asked what his favorite hymn was. His reply was "In the Garden." I made note of that and decided right then I would never forget it. To this day, whenever I hear that song or sing it, I remember that encounter from well over forty years ago.

A few years later when we had moved to Florida to pastor a church, that same little old lady would send my parents the bulletin from the church in Pennsylvania. Why do I remember this? Because she always taped three sticks of gum on the inside of the bulletin for my sisters and me. I remember running out to fetch the mail every week looking to intercept that delicious-smelling envelope. I also remember when those bulletins stopped coming. Though she had passed, her memory and kindness lingered.

There are a lot of memories I have from my early childhood. The one that stuck out the most was the never-ending struggles we faced. Growing up as a pastor's kid in the mid to late 1970s and 1980s was challenging. My dad was not paid much money, and my mom was not able to work much outside the home because she was caring for me and my sisters. She had to become very resourceful to meet the needs of our family with what little money my dad made.

I remember wearing matching dresses she had sewn for us from fabric she had either recycled, or my grandma had given her. I remember sitting on a bucket in the garden snapping beans, shelling peas, and eyeing potatoes in the cold cellar. Oh, I hated the cellar! I was so terrified of that cold, dark, damp basement. Still gives me the creeps!

I remember watching my mom sew curtains for the house, helping her do laundry with the ringer washer in the basement, hanging clothes on the clothesline to dry, and then folding those crispy fibers when they were taken down.

She spent many days baking never-ending mounds of gobs and cream puffs with her best friend. That was always a good day!

I remember her preparing deer and other wild game with my grandma after the men had brought home their kill. I remember my mom sending us to the little old lady's house across the street from our home to pick apples and grapes.

I remember being part of the family gathering to harvest all the sweet corn from the garden. I am talking hay wagons full of corn! I remember one time we had so much corn, that my Pappy called all the town folk to come and get as much corn as they wanted for free. I remember sitting next to a family friend and farm hand at the picnic table overlooking my Pappy's pond, eating corn on the cob, while giggling because I had had a crush on him since I was a toddler.

I learned so many life skills by just watching my mom do life in the garden and kitchen, and my dad do ministry. Some of the sweetest life lessons I learned were with my dad. I was a Daddy's girl—his firstborn. While my parents always said I got the best of both of them, I think I am a lot like my dad. I have become more and more like my Daddy every day; from the sentimental side of crying in church almost every Sunday, to my gypsy-like spirit that could go anywhere or live anywhere in the world and enjoy every second of it. He taught me to love music—especially hymns. He and I used to sing duets together in church when I was a teenager. I talked to my dad anytime I had struggles in life. He was always ready to listen and offer up godly advice by quoting several verses to me regularly:

"Trust in the Lord with all your heart and lean not on your own understanding; in all your ways submit to him, and he will direct your paths." Proverbs 3:5-6

"What then shall we say in response to these things? If God is for us, who can be against us?" Romans 8:31

"Have I not commanded you? Be strong and courageous. Do not be afraid; do not be discouraged, for the Lord God will be with you wherever you go." Joshua 1:9

"And My God will meet all your needs according to the riches of his glory in Christ Jesus." Philippians 4:19

"Trust and obey, for there is no other way; to be happy in Jesus but to trust and obey." ~John H Sammins, 1887 (Proverbs 3:5-6; Philippians 4:6-7)

As a young girl, wrestling through common life battles, I needed to hear these wise words of wisdom—lovingly and repeatedly. My dad always had a way of making me feel safe and secure in his loving arms and godly counsel.

We live in a world today that is full of empty words and sayings, self-talk, inspirational quotes, little quips that sound right, man's logic and reasoning, and so on. We repeat phrases like *"Keep Calm and Carry On"*, *"Don't Worry, Be Happy"* or *"What would Jesus do?"*, never really arriving at a state of peace, nor often doing what Jesus told us to do.

Creator God's Word is powerful and holds the secrets to life's battles. He told us to trust Him with all our hearts, not to rely on our own understanding of the situation, but rather submit to Him. He told us He would lead us down the right paths by the working of the Spirit. He told us to be courageous and strong and to rest knowing He will give us what we need. We just have to trust and obey.

We certainly need more people in our lives who will listen to our pain and offer godly wisdom by presenting us with Scripture to cling to. However, what we need is more time to be still and to listen for the Spirit to lead.

As you read through this book, I hope you find ways you can practice being still and listening. I hope that you will begin to hear his voice a little louder in your soul. It is a still small voice. Even a pin dropping to the floor in a silent auditorium can be heard. Silencing our minds and hearts is the key to augmenting His still small voice.

One of the ways I have chosen to practice being still is through daily quiet moments on my front or back porch with my morning cup of coffee. I turn on Native American flute music, burn some sage, and close my eyes. As I listen to the sounds of nature, feel the gentle breeze, and inhale the aroma of the fresh air, I try to sit as still as possible and block out all distractions. Sometimes, I drift back to an almost sleep-like state, but usually, I just wait for the Creator to meet me in that space. He always speaks softly and sweetly. I love these moments in the early mornings while the earth is still quietly awakening. I find this sets my mind and soul for the day. Over time, I have found that I am less quick to react to stress in life and feel more peace in my heart.

Questions to Ponder:

What are some of your fondest memories from childhood?

What are some life skills you learned by simply watching your parents or grandparents perform them?

Think back to a time in your life when you struggled as a child growing up. Was there an adult in your life that you ran to for wisdom and guidance? Did you feel safe with them?

As an adult, are you that person for someone else?

Do you often give yourself time to get still and meditate and listen for the voice of Creator God?

What is something in your life that could benefit from getting quiet and allowing Creator to speak?

What are 3 ways you can practice being still and listening for Creator to speak to you?

Are you willing to be strong & courageous? Are you willing to trust & obey?

Is your soul awakening?

CHOICES

*"Rise and shine, Morning Glory!
It's time to get up!"*

—Dad

Oh, how I did not appreciate those morning wake-up calls from my dad! I mean really, what young teenager likes to be abruptly roused by a chipper morning person, not to mention a parent? It certainly did not set the tone for me to be in a sunshiny mood at 6:30 am on school days. However, as much as this night owl hated mornings, I look back on those moments with fondness.

As an adult, I can now appreciate his eagerness for the day and the joy he always exuded in life. So much so, I became the parent my dad was to me.

As I am writing this, I am belly laughing with tears rolling down my face because I am reminded of another phrase he always said and still says to me, "You're becoming more and more like your Daddy every day!" No matter how hard I tried not to, I did.

(still laughing)

I can recount many ways that I "tortured" my children with funny phrases and made-up morning wake-up songs as they were growing up—just like my dad. I even recall a middle school assignment my oldest daughter had to write describing things she likes about her mom and dad. One of the things she wrote was how she likes it when her mom sings "Get up" to the tune of "Jingle Bells" (wait for it) with my dramatic soprano opera voice. She never ever ever EVER showed that she liked it, but deep down that obnoxious song created fond memories of her annoying chipper (still not a morning glory) mom. While my daughter may never sing that song to her children, I have a feeling my oldest son will, because as my dad says, "he's becoming more and more like his Pappy every day!" Boy is he! I would say that I feel sorry for my granddaughter, but nah, those will be good memories for her—someday.

(still laughing)

Childhood memories. For good or bad, we all have them. We can all remember times in our early lives that tickled our funny bones, made us squeal with excitement, and yes, even times we do not care to recall. Life is full of them. From the time we enter this world until we depart, we make memories.

I would like to say only the good times are the ones that shape us. Unfortunately, that is not true. Sometimes bad experiences harm us deeply. Out of a need to self-protect, we cover them up and move on quickly. After all, we cannot afford to lose time grieving or tending to a wound. We have been taught to pull ourselves up by our bootstraps and get on with the rest of life. As the saying goes, "Suck it up, buttercup!"

Left unattended over time, these wounds become infected and putrid, rearing their ugly heads in a variety of ways in our lives. These old wounds affect every aspect of our lives no matter how hard we try to avoid them. From how we relate to our spouse, children, parents, extended family, friends, employees or colleagues, neighbors, and church, everyone is affected by our life experiences—for good or bad.

If you do not think this to be true, then look at the state of the world today. The family unit is a wreck. Children are not just fatherless, but also motherless and in too many cases orphaned. Local and federal government corruption affects all of us in more ways than we can count. It seems each generation of leaders is more corrupt than the one that came before.

Bringing it even closer to home, when one parent makes a decision (good or bad), their spouse and children are affected. Focusing even closer to home, when you make poor lifestyle choices, your very body is affected. Going even deeper, your future children are affected. Yep —even your children and grandchildren who are not yet born are affected!

Did you know not only do your lifestyle choices today affect the DNA structure of your future children, but you are carrying DNA formed by the lifestyle choices of your mother, father, grandfathers, and grandmothers? Native American culture teaches that your actions affect the next seven generations of your descendants.

Guess what! Science has even proved that "stress" changes your DNA expression. A systematic review conducted by the BMC Medical Genetics research team found that exposure to stress can modify how DNA activates, which may alter gene expression and therefore contribute to disease composition. (Muka T, 2016;212:174-83) What all that means is that your genes can be altered by stress and contribute to the cause of chronic disease. This has an impact not only on your current health but when your DNA is altered your reproductive cells are also altered, making your future offspring more susceptible to chronic disease—and I'll add, for the next seven generations.

In chiropractic, we define stress as your mental, emotional, physical, and spiritual response to trauma, toxins, and thoughts. Stress triggers a neurological response in your body to create inflammation. Inflammation is the cause of all discomfort, illness, and disease. So good stress as well as bad stress creates neurological responses in the central nervous system. The bad stress creates changes in the proper function of cells, soft tissues, organs, and the skeleton. If the body doesn't function well, inflammation is sure to ensue. The inflammation is followed by pain and disease when left untreated.

If you still are not convinced that your life choices impact others, consider the story of Moses' second trip up Mount Sinai after having already received the Ten Commandments.

The first time Moses went up to Mount Sinai he expressed to the Lord that he was unsure how the Hebrew people would know that God would lead them into the Promised Land. Moses wanted a sign to know that Presence was guiding them. So, the Lord sent Moses up the mountain a second time. This time, the Lord hid Moses in the cleft of a rock and shielded Him with His hand while His Glory passed by. Then He removed His hand so Moses could see his back, but His face could not be seen. This was because the glory of the Lord is so powerful anyone who looks directly upon the face of God would die instantly. As the glory of the Lord passed by, this is what The Lord said,

"'The Lord, the Lord, the compassionate and gracious God, slow to anger, abounding in love and faithfulness, maintaining love to thousands, and forgiving wickedness, rebellion, and sin. Yet he does not leave the guilty unpunished; he punishes the children and their children for the sins of the parents to the third and fourth generation.' Moses bowed to the ground at once and worshiped. 'Lord', he said 'if I have found favor in your eyes, then let the Lord go

with us. Although this is a stiff-necked people, forgive our sin, and take us as your inheritance'" Exodus 34:6-9.

When Moses came back down the mountain, he was not aware that his face was glowing after he had spoken with the Lord. At first, everyone was afraid to go near him. Moses had already given them the Ten Commandments, but they had ignored God and were committing idolatry at the foot of the mountain worshiping a golden calf. Moses smashed the tablets upon seeing this and then he goes back to God to ask for forgiveness. Then God reveals his Glory to Moses. At this point, Moses re-makes the tablets and restores the covenant. From then on, Moses wore a veil when he would speak to the people after being with the Lord because the Glory of the Lord was still radiating from him.

After that time, when Moses would go up the mountain to speak to the Lord, he would remove the veil. When he returned to the people, he would cover his face again. This was so the people knew he had been speaking to the Lord. This was the sign Moses had asked for.

We could take a deep dive into the story of Moses on Mount Sinai, but for the sake of this chapter, I just want to zero in on one specific statement the Lord says to Moses. He is a *"compassionate and gracious God, slow to anger, abounding in love and faithfulness, maintaining love to thousands, and forgiving wickedness, rebellion, and sin. Yet he does not leave the guilty unpunished; he punishes his children and their children for the sins of the parents to the third and fourth generations."*

Some scholars believe this is only referring to their immediate household because it was the custom for generations of a single family to live in one home. One parent's actions would have an impact on the entire household.

However, science has proven, that while this assertion is certainly true, epigenetics (outside influences) have a profound impact on our DNA expression and that of our future children and generations to come unless something changes. In this case, I think science has proven a mystery in the Bible for how this passing down of sin happens biologically.

I do not think many will argue how the impact of having a parent who suffers from addiction affects not only the emotional health of the family, but their children are also prone to addiction. This is the impact of DNA and the judgment of God.

But there is hope!

Have you also heard or even said these words? "The buck stops here." Or "It ends with me." The reality is that while this punishment is passed down, our Creator in all his compassion, grace, love, and faithfulness; is ready and willing to forgive wickedness, rebellion, and sin in our lives. In His forgiveness, He wipes the slate clean, so we can change the trajectory for not only ourselves but also for our children and future generations.

While you may have had a great or a not-so-great childhood, you get to decide the life you give to your children and your descendants. Maybe there is something you are responsible for that is affecting your relationships. Consider a change of course, so that one day you might hear your child tell your grandchild, "You're becoming more and more like your grandma/grandpa every day." Better yet, "You're becoming more and more like your Creator Father every day!"

Questions to Ponder:

What are some fond memories you have that shaped you to become "more and more like your mom or dad every day?"

What are some good traits that you have fostered in your life and would like to pass on to your children or grandchildren?

What are some characteristics, health challenges, and lifestyle choices you are not proud of?

Are you willing to seek forgiveness and change course for the betterment of your descendants?

Is your soul awakening?

SANCTIFICATION

"It is well with my soul."

—Horatio Spafford, 1873

As with every year for the last several years, in 2023, I asked Creator God to reveal to me the verse He would have for me to meditate on. I do this in place of resolutions because they just do not work for me. I try hard, but no matter what, I have always struggled to memorize Scripture. Maybe it is bad memories of weekly Christian middle school Bible verse tests that I rarely passed?

I mentioned in the Introduction that I am not afraid of failure. To overcome failure and manage stress, I choose to succeed by asking Creator to give me a verse that will cause me to focus on Him regularly throughout the year. For the last several years He has done that. During times of joy, sadness, triumph, and loss, no matter the situation, He regularly reminds me of the verse(s) He has chosen for me that year. It is such a cool way He affirms to me He is there and listening. When December rolls around and He reveals the meditation for the upcoming year, I usually respond with "Wow! Cool! This is such a great verse for me and I'm eager to see what the year holds." Each year proves to reflect the verse or verses He gave me.

The first year I began the practice of meditating on a single verse was in 2014 when I was a recent graduate from chiropractic school. I have done so every year since.

In December 2022, the Great Spirit gave me His Word that year, but I did not receive it well. It felt more like a punch in the gut. I was downright stunned and frankly, angry because what He gave me seemed to be a prediction of a very hard year to come. It took me about two weeks to process it. I had many questions, thoughts, and emotions that were unleashed swirling like flames of fire through my mind.

Most years He has given me one verse. A couple of times he has given me two. Those were tough years. But that December, He gave me three! He also gave me four words and a song. If you're like me, you're probably reading this like "Wow! I'm surprised by that response. Angry at God? What is up, doc? Where is your faith? Where is your joy? *Where is your hope and peace?*" Yeah, it was a surprise to me too.

The first verse the Spirit gave me has been my life verse since I was in elementary school. I have recited that verse countless times in my life. You will recall, it was one of the verses my dad quoted to me as a child. If you asked my children today what my favorite verse is they would say Joshua 1:9.

> *"Have I not commanded you? Be strong and courageous. Do not be afraid; do not be discouraged, for the Lord God will be with you wherever you go." Joshua 1:9 NIV*

The second verse the Spirit gave me is another verse my dad quoted to me all the time when I struggled with life stuff growing up.

> *"Trust in the Lord with all your heart and lean not on your own understanding; in all your ways submit to him, and he will direct your paths." Proverbs 3:5-6 NIV*

The third verse the Spirit gave me, feels like He is putting a huge exclamation point at the end of those previous verses.

"For the Word of God will never fail." Luke 1:37 NIV

The song he gave me that year, came to me in a dream one Sunday morning before Christmas. In my dream, I was singing the hymn "It is Well with My Soul." When I woke up, I wondered why I was singing that song and if we would be singing it in the worship service that morning.

Well, as luck would have it, we did sing it in church and the pastor referenced all three of the verses God revealed to me in his sermon that morning. "Umm, ok God, you have got my attention! ALL three verses are for me this year. But that song too? Gulp! What on earth will this year hold?"

During the worship portion of that Sunday morning service, I got a text message from my dad letting me know he and his siblings had taken my grandpa off life support and were preparing to meet Jesus. Wow! Ok, not the kind of text you want to receive in church. "It is well with my soul" seemed like a fitting prayer that day.

The four words the Spirit gave me for 2023 were: Connection (with Creator), Alignment (with Truth), Health, and Strength.

While I am normally eager and excited to see what the new year holds for me, I entered 2023 with fear and trepidation. I am not afraid of challenges, but I am tired.

You see, in January 2022 I suddenly became very sick. I had contracted a bad case of Covid. I had to resign from my job and spent most of that year in tremendous pain. Once I was no longer contagious, long-haul Covid set in and lasted the entire year. I spent thousands of dollars and countless hours in therapy to regain normal brain function so that I could even walk again. The hardest part of my recovery was none of my symptoms were visible. While I looked fine, I was far from well. After nearly one full year of determination, I was finally getting back to my badass self.

The year 2022 was so very hard! So, you can imagine how hard it was for me to think 2023 was going to be just as hard or even harder; considering the verses, song, and words the Spirit gave me to meditate on.

I say all this because I am tired of the fake smiley facades we parade around pretending to have it all together when maybe we are confused, annoyed, frustrated, upset, angry, or just plain tired. Why is it we must appear perfect to have a good testimony to the broken world? That is ridiculous! In the end, we just look like clowns and are so pious in our attitudes. No one is perfect—not one single person, but we are made perfect by the redeeming blood of Jesus. It is His blood that cleansed us and made us white as snow.

But one word… sanctification.

That is a big word that means the daily working out of our faith so that we look more and more like Jesus. It is a process that will be completed when Creator Father calls us home. In the meantime, we are being shaped and molded. It is not easy and is often painful. Sanctification is the part that builds character and strength under fire— the purifying process.

Through the daily grind, the good, the bad, the ugly, the raw, the REAL, we grow and become stronger. Even though we screw up, and have bad days, and ugly moments; through His son, Jesus, Creator God still declares us perfect.

While I was not feeling it with these verses at the start of 2022, it's ok. It's ok to be authentic, real, and honest; yet still be a Jesus follower. It is ok to struggle, wrestle, and go through seasons of not feeling it. It is ok to be frustrated, confused, and even angry with God.

However, in those times of turmoil, remember He is still God and He still loves you more than you can ever imagine. You are still His perfect child. He is always there and will hold you up with his right hand. It will be ok. It does not mean you have less faith or that you are walking away from Creator God. It just means you are human. That is where God loves to meet us—in our humanity.

So, even when my strength fails and my heart breaks, with all that is left in me I will say, "It is well with my soul." because the Word of God never fails. Therefore, I will trust in the Lord with all my heart, not lean on my own understanding, acknowledge Him in all I do, and choose to be strong and courageous. He has promised He will guide me in the right direction.

Update on 2023: It turned out to be a great year with so many blessings following a LOT of hard work. So, I may have overreacted when God gave me those verses for 2023. I certainly needed all the strength I could muster too. But you know what? He knew that and loved me despite my weakness, frailness, and unknowing.

Questions to Ponder:

Have you ever been angry or disappointed with God?

How did you respond? Did you ever come around and see through His eyes what He had planned for you?

Do you think Creator God still loves you when you are disappointed with him?

Do you think He is upset with you when you are angry with him?

How have you been allowing Creator God to purify your life as you allow Him to lead your life?

Is your soul awakening?

REFINER'S FIRE

"Oh, beautiful for spacious skies,
For amber waves of grain,
For purple mountains majesties
Above the fruited plain!
America! America!
God shed His grace on thee,
And crown thy good with brotherhood
From sea to shining sea."

—Katherine Lee Bates, 1893

It is the last week of July 2008. Our newly renovated late 1800s Italian Village home in The Short North of Columbus, Ohio sold in two days. Thirty days later the house was empty, and the family minivan was packed floor to ceiling and tied down on the roof—a covered wagon experience. We looked like the Clampetts in the Beverly Hillbillies driving our wagon across the country to the land of cement rivers and concrete jungles. Except we had *not* struck gold. We barely had two nickels to rub together. It was just Mike and I plus four kids under the age of eleven setting off on a seven-day journey to the wild-wild west of Southern California. We had snacks and a few bucks for burgers and fries along the way.

Despite the market crash of 2008, feeling desperately broke, the escalating gas prices, having just a few pennies to rub together, no place to put our feet inside the van, horrible nights trying to sleep in roach motels, food cravings for anything but junk-food and the sweltering heat of the midwestern plains; we made some awesome memories on that trip! I had been homeschooling the kids for a year before we moved. Part of their curriculum was working through a monthly children's state workbook and maps. We had collected all fifty states. Their assignment, while traveling west, was to read and color through each state we traversed. It surely kept them busy and was a fun activity for them—for like ten minutes!

Through Ohio and Illinois, we played "I Spy" and "The License Plate Game" until we got to the plains of Missouri and Kansas. There were no more cars on the highway; just hot, humid, and barren land. Not much to spy on and not another license plate for at least one hundred miles!

Suddenly, in the middle of Kansas, our nine-year-old son let out the loudest, most blood-curdling gasp! My husband slammed on the brakes, sending me into a momentary panic. I whipped around in the front passenger seat and *nicely* screamed "What's wrong?" Our son replies in his surprised nine-year-old voice, "The road is turning!" If he had not been three rows back with a mound of fast-food bags, two hundred stuffed animals, a basketball, two chess boards, thirteen hundred duffle bags, and a sleeping toddler in a car seat; he might have been left on the side of the road! Once our blood pressure returned to normal, we all started laughing uncontrollably because it *was* hilarious. Interstate 70 across the Midwest plains is nothing but a straight road to nowhere. The kids renamed the state of Missouri to "Misery."

We tried to stop and see a couple of sites, but the humidity and heat were crushing. We were all miserable. So, what else do you do in July with a van load of elementary-aged kids on a cross-country moving trip except get to your destination as quickly as possible?

By the time we got to Arizona, the desert heat was a whopping 115F and dry enough to suck every drop of liquid out of your body! A couple rode up on their motorcycles, wearing their leathers. While leather usually helps keep you cool on a bike in the summer, they were boiling. They jumped off their bikes at the gas station, opened the ice cooler outside the front door, and threw their jackets into the giant ice chest before going inside to use the bathroom and grab several bottles of water. It was just *that* hot and just *that* miserable of a stretch of highway for hundreds and hundreds of miles.

An unforgettable memory stands out to me. I vividly saw the song "America the Beautiful" come to life! I now know exactly what inspired Katherine Lee Bates to write her poem while on her trip to Pikes Peak in 1893.

Those spacious skies and amber waves of grain are the Midwest states of Ohio, Illinois, Kansas, and Missouri. In the summer before harvest, the wheatgrass turns amber brown. As the wind blows across the plains, the fruit of grain fields ripple back and forth like ocean waves. The purple mountains majesty? As you're approaching the Colorado Rockies from the fruited plains, the mountain range appears purple, just like the Blue Ridge mountains appear blue upon approach. It is truly one of the most majestic things I've ever experienced.

Life is a lot like this road trip, isn't it? All the clutter and mess are closing in all around. So many demands and never enough money to make our corner of the world go around. It is hot, man, like real hot. Relationship struggles with our significant others are sucking the energy right out of us. The never-ending "To-Do list" leaves us sweating like pigs and utterly exhausted. Then suddenly, like out of nowhere a loud clap of lightning flashes across the sky, the thunder rolls, and panic sets in. Are the car windows closed? What is outside that cannot get wet? Where is the dog? Before you know it, it is pouring down rain. I mean it is a real gusher. The storm is on top of you howling and growling like a wild animal.

Just as quickly as it comes, it ends. The sun comes out and the majesty of a crystal-clear blue sky accompanied by the smell of fresh clean air overcomes your senses. Life is good again.

As you will recall, I am a trained opera singer. One of my favorite arias is a bass solo in the oratorio by G.F. Handel, *The Messiah* "Who May Abide the Day of His

Coming—For He is Like a Refiner's Fire." It's based on Malachi 3:2 that reads,

> "But who can endure the day of his coming? Who can stand when he appears? For he will be like a refiner's fire or a launderer's soap. He will sit as a refiner and purify the Levites and refine them like gold and silver. Then the Lord will have men who will bring offerings in righteousness, and the offerings of Judah and Jerusalem will be acceptable to the Lord, as in days gone by, as in former days." Malachi 3:2-4 NIV

Here is the lesson. Unless you go through the fire, you cannot be purified. Without purification, you cannot stand before the Most Holy Creator. Gold is not much to look at until it is put under intense pressure and heat in a refiner's fire. Once it goes through the purification process, it comes out on the other side shining like the beautiful pure gold we adorn our ears, fingers, wrists, and necks with.

In the same way, the struggles we go through in this life are designed to purify our hearts and minds so that when we meet Creator God we can be presented as pure gold! The chiseling, heat, pressure, pain, and sorrow we go through on this earth is nothing compared to the immense joy we will experience when we enter the presence of the Great Spirit.

The next time you are struggling through something, try to remember you are being refined. While it certainly is not enjoyable whatsoever, changing your perspective a little can help to ease the pain of suffering.

To close out this chapter, click over to your favorite audio streaming app and listen to this alto and soprano aria from The Messiah. It is so beautiful and will surely calm your soul: "He Shall Feed His Flock Like a Shepherd" from *The Messiah* performed by The Mormon Tabernacle Choir at Temple Square 2016. May Creator God bless you and comfort you in your struggles.

Questions to Ponder:

Was there a time in your life when something majestic you had read about or had seen pictures of came to life for you?

How did that experience change the way you think about that place?

Is there a song that reminds you of a moment in life that speaks to you?

What has been your favorite road trip to date?

Did everything go as planned?

What are some of the experiences you have never forgotten from that trip?

Looking back, have you been able to shed some light on those not-so-great moments? Do you see the lesson learned?

Is there a battle raging in your life right now? What is a way you can remind yourself that you are being refined and purified?

Is your soul awakening?

CHANGE

"Change is easy.
Thinking about change is hard."

—Eric Plasker, DC

Twenty years ago, I was a young mom working as a chiropractic assistant. I loved working in that chiropractic office in Columbus, Ohio. It was such an eye-opening experience for me to watch people's lives be radically changed by the healing they experienced through chiropractic care. I saw a deaf patient regain her hearing. I saw a young woman crippled by an autoimmune condition completely heal and walk again, later to become a corrections officer at the women's state penitentiary. I saw a cranky elderly lady who walked hunched over at nearly a 45-degree angle straighten up and become such a pleasant and funny patient. What I witnessed, because people decided it was time to change their health, was truly miraculous!

I was invited to accompany the doctors and the rest of the staff to a chiropractic seminar in Boston. I was excited to be invited because my desire to maybe become a chiropractor someday was growing.

One of the speakers was Dr. Eric Plasker, a well-known chiropractor and mentor within the chiropractic industry. He gave a talk about living to over one hundred years old. His talk was very insightful and motivating. He described how medical advances have made it possible for people to live to one hundred years of age. However, he drilled it home how *quality* of years is more important than *quantity*. I still remember one of his statements that hit home with me that day: "Change is easy. Thinking about change is hard."

I remember thinking to myself, "What did he just say? Change isn't easy?! Ha! Change is HARD!"

He went on to clarify that we spend a good deal of time thinking about and stressing over the *thought* of making a change. However, the *act* of making that change is quite easy. He closed by reminding us once again that what matters is the quality of life we live in those one hundred years. For most of us, that will require us to change our mindsets, lifestyles, diets, relationships, priorities, and values. No one wants to live one hundred years sick, broke, dying, and all alone. Change is easy. Thinking about change is hard.

Let me give you an example, if you are headed south on a two-lane road in the middle of nowhere, and miss your turn, what do you do? You turn the car around and go back. Changing course is easy.

Now, if you are headed south on that two-lane road while cutting it close on your way to a meeting and miss your turn, what is your reaction? I am going to go out on a limb here and suspect your reaction would go something like this:

"Ah, man! (smacking the steering wheel) I missed my turn! I was so distracted by that argument I had with my colleague before I left the office, I didn't notice my turn. (checking the rear-view mirror) Grrr, I have a tractor-trailer riding my tail or I'd whip into that next driveway. The next street is like one hundred miles down the road. Ugh! There goes half a tank of gas at these ridiculous prices. Fine! I'll put on my blinker to warn this dude I'm slowing down and look for a place to turn around. He better get off my tail. Oh bless, there's a driveway! (Now looking in the rearview mirror to back out onto the road) Seriously?!?! Of course, there had to be ten cars coming from the other direction! I'm surely going to be late for that meeting with a potential client. Let's hope I don't lose the contract. (headache begins

to set in). Finally, I can get back on track. Oh, my aching head! Maybe I'll get there on time if I drive fast enough."

Now what was harder? Turning around and getting back on track or the entire internal dialogue you just had over having to turn around and the headache you just induced? Change is easy. Thinking about change is hard.

You might be familiar with the story in the Bible of Jonah and the Whale. Jonah was a prophet of Israel during the reign of Jeroboam II in the mid-700s BC. (English Standard Version, 2001-2004 Crossway) The Lord came to Jonah and told him to go to the wicked and dangerous city of Nineveh. Jonah knew how evil Nineveh was. He was afraid of these people. Instead of obeying Creator God, he chose to run away.

In Joppa, he rented a boat to take him to Tarshish. While on board, God sent a violent storm that terrified the sailors. To lighten the ship, they began throwing cargo into the sea.

The captain went looking for Jonah and found him below deck in a deep sleep. He woke Jonah and told him to call on his god that maybe he would have mercy and save them.

The crew was so afraid they began to cast lots to determine who angered the gods. The lot fell on Jonah, so they demanded he explain himself. He explained he was a Hebrew and worshiped the God of heaven and earth, who made the sea and the dry land. The crew exclaimed asking him what he had done because he had already told them he was running away from the Great Spirit.

The storm was getting worse. Jonah, knowing this was all his fault, told the crew to throw him into the sea. The men refused because it was too dangerous. They tried to row back to land, but the storm only got worse. So, the men begged the Great Spirit to not hold them responsible for killing a man and then threw Jonah into the sea, where he was swallowed by a huge fish (we like to think it was a whale). Promptly, the sea calmed.

Jonah was in the belly of the fish for three days and three nights where Jonah cried out to the Creator, lamenting his disobedience, and vowing to go to Nineveh to declare the Salvation of the Lord. Right away the fish spit Jonah out onto dry land.

The Creator told Jonah a second time to go to the wicked city of Nineveh to proclaim the message He had given him. This time Jonah obeyed. When he arrived, the wicked people of Nineveh, whom Jonah feared, listened to, and obeyed the message from God, including the King!

Prophets are often the most rejected message bearers from Creator God. No one likes to hear they are doing wrong and need to change their ways. No one wants to hear a message of tragedy being foretold. Why do you think that is? Because thinking about change is hard!

Jonah did not want to go to the evil city of Nineveh to deliver a message of repentance. This was a million-against-one kind of situation. He was afraid they would kill him. Instead, he chose to run away from the Great Spirit—and we see how that turned out.

When he finally obeyed, He discovered every single person in the city including the tiniest of babies, even the King himself, was not only *ready* for change, but the King also proclaimed a fast across the entire city including the animals. He proclaimed everyone should call on God, to repent and turn from their evil and violence.

When Creator God saw what the people did, he relented and did not destroy the people like he had threatened. Had Jonah just obeyed the Great Spirit from the beginning, he would not have had to go through so much turmoil, and who knows how many people's lives could have been spared from the hands of the Ninevites, while Jonah was running from Creator.

Yes, change is easy. <u>Thinking</u> about change is hard!

Questions to Ponder:

What do you think? Do you agree with this statement, "Change is easy. Thinking about change is hard?"

What is something in your life that needs to change, but you have been putting off due to the internal dialogue in your head?

How much more difficult do you think you are making the process of change by throwing out all the reasons you can't change?

Imagine what your life will look like if you make this change.

Can you see a brighter future because of this change?

Is your soul awakening?

PAIN

Grief, after the initial shock of loss,
comes in waves…
When you're driving alone in your car.
While you're doing the dishes.
While you are getting ready for work…
All of a sudden it hits you —
how so very much you miss someone,
and your breath catches,
and your tears flow,
and the sadness is so great
that it's physically painful."

—Nicole Gabert

In 2009, at the age of thirty-eight with four children under the age of ten, having just moved to California for my husband's ministry, I started back to school to become a chiropractor. Five years of grueling education, five hundred exams (not an exaggeration), three internships, five National Board exams, and the California state licensure exam later; I became a Doctor of Chiropractic. Whew! I made it!

After graduation, I launched my private practice with two thousand dollars and some change. I worked tirelessly to grow my practice in California. Every weekend, I attended an event somewhere to meet prospective patients. When I passed the three-year mark, I was elated to have beat the statistics that say most small businesses close in the first three years.

During year four of practice, I was exhausted and lonely. My husband and kids were all I had. I did not have many friends since graduating from school, as they all scattered around the country to start their new jobs or open their practices. I felt like all I did was work and sleep.

The icing on the cake came in the form of a giant dagger to my gut. One evening after work I decided to set aside exhaustion and attend a dinner with my husband and several other couples from our church. Sitting around the table enjoying the night, I was joking around with one of the men. I am a die-hard Ohio State Buckeye, while he was a die-hard Michigan Wolverine. We were laughing and bantering with each other—the typical sports bantering. Anyone who knows The Ohio State v. Michigan rivalry understands it is the biggest and most intense rivalry in all of sports—ALL sports! Therefore, good-natured bantering is expected and welcomed.

Suddenly, the host stands up, pointing at me, and proclaims loudly "And this is why we don't invite Mindi to anything." *(insert dagger & cue laughter from all in attendance)* In utter disbelief and profound pain, I turned to my husband and quietly stated "I'm leaving." At that, I got up and left the dinner. I drove home bawling my eyes out and went straight to bed.

After that gut-wrenching and humiliating event, I became incredibly introverted and terrified of going places outside of work. I began having mild to severe panic attacks. Work was safe for me. So, I plugged away enjoying every minute I spent with patients.

As soon as I finished working for the day, panic would set in again. I would not go anywhere for fear of running into people I might know. When we did go out, I clung to my husband's arm like a terrified child and did not stay long.

That fall, a colleague and I decided to attend a chiropractic convention in Orlando, Florida. I grew up in Clearwater and was thrilled to head back to my old stomping grounds and maybe even get a chance to see my best friend from middle school. I had not seen her since 1989. Thanks to social media, we had reconnected for several years.

The day came for my flight to the Sunshine State. I was elated with excitement! I kissed my husband goodbye, jumped on an airplane, and set off to meet my old childhood friend for breakfast upon arrival. What a sweet and blessed time that was for the two of us. We hadn't seen each other in over thirty years. Yet, it was like we hadn't spent a day apart. We talked for hours. Before we departed, she invited me to see the restaurant she owned when it opened for service later that morning.

In the meantime, I drove around Clearwater, Dunedin, Palm Harbor, and Tarpon Springs admiring how things were still the same; yet how many things had changed. The sunshine, freedom, salty ocean air, and humidity were such a welcome pleasure compared to the arid, dry heat of Los Angeles.

I drove past the home I grew up in. So many memories of Lake Shore Drive. Oh, to turn back time! I dreamed about how maybe one day I could purchase my old home, renovate it, and return to life on Lake Tarpon. I haven't given up on that dream.

From there I stopped at the church my dad had pastored back then. It still looked the same. Such a beautiful stone facade with a white steeple, tucked back into the woods. Locals called it "The Church in the Wildwood." It was the most incredible church I had ever been part of. On this day, I missed the people of that little Church in the Wildwood more than ever. However, it is an entirely different congregation now.

It was nearing time to meet my best friend, but I still had a bit of time. I drove to Dunedin causeway and pulled my car right out onto the sandy strip. I always thought that was the coolest thing about the Dunedin Causeway. Both sides of the strip are designed for boat launching, fishing, jet-skiing, and other water sports. As I stepped into the water, I watched as the waves gently lapped across my feet. Looking up, I inhaled deeply and gazed up at the beautiful blue sky. I was home! *(exhale)*

At that moment, out of nowhere a tsunami of childhood memories flashed before my eyes and took the wind right out of me. With one huge wail, I exploded in tears. So many memories—some I cherished but buried deep within to protect from all harm. While others I put out of my mind never to be unearthed again. Course-changing decisions were made because of those experiences. I was not ready to face those memories. To top it all off, I was just told in no uncertain words that I was not welcome in my church community where my husband was a pastor!

As I stood in the water, tears flowing, Creator wrapped His loving arms around me and comforted me. There were no words exchanged. He just let me cry.

I composed myself to meet my friend again. We had lunch together and enjoyed sharing more stories, laughter, and memories. A little while later, much to my dismay, it was time for me to head to Orlando for the opening of the convention. I do not remember much from that convention, to be honest. My mind was in Clearwater. I had one more person I needed to see.

So, I made the call and ditched the last morning of the convention. We met for breakfast in Orlando and enjoyed several hours together catching up on lost time. The walls I had built around my heart began to crack. "Do not break, Mindi. Do not break. Keep it all together. God, please help me keep it all together!"

I could not.

As if time had never passed, I freely spoke, and my heart shattered like mosaic glass into millions of pieces. While it had been a lifetime of water under the bridge, my old friend and I shared a heartfelt moment of compassion that I will never forget.

I remember sitting in the Orlando airport begging God to cancel my flight. I did not want to leave. "Please God, don't make me go back to California. I never wanted to leave Florida all those years ago. I wanted to stay. I had a life I wanted to live in Florida. Why did you move me to Indiana all those years ago?"

The flight was delayed. "Could this be the answer?" Then delayed again. "Oh Great Spirit, please! Let me stay!"

Boarding time arrived.

With crushing obedience, I took my seat on the plane, staring out the window into the night sky and city lights below, in stone-cold silence with tears streaming down my cheeks the entire flight home.

When my husband picked me up at the airport, I tried to shove my emotions down and smile, but he knew I was struggling. He knew I had faced some very deep anguish on my trip. He tried to make small talk, but it was useless.

We stopped for food at our favorite California burger joint, as is our traditional airport escapade. Not even their famous burgers and monstrous fries helped. I stared out the truck window for the rest of the drive home.

On top of feeling unloved, unacceptable, and completely unworthy; I also felt gutted like a fish. Creator ushered in a four-year grieving process.

The problem was I had no one to talk to. While I was busy in practice, I was working to pay the bills. There was not anything left over for grief counseling. I did not trust anyone I knew either. I certainly did *not* trust any of the local pastors, elders, their wives, or church counselors with my heart.

I was working with a business coach at the time. She shifted gears and became my life coach. I thank God every single day for my coach and the incredible grace, love, and kick-in-the-pants mentoring she gave to me. She walked alongside me as I grieved and worked through the pain. Not long after I returned from Florida, I decided I was leaving California—with or without my husband—yikes! So, I set to create a two-year exit plan.

That year was unreal. The panic was awful. The tears were constant. The sleepless nights and grief were unbearable. I spent countless days and nights at the jetty on Seal Beach and in the Joshua Tree Desert crying out to Creator, begging Him for healing. I was spiraling and nothing was working to overcome the incredible grief I was going through. In true inner-battle fashion, I looked fine on the outside, but I was far from okay.

All those years ago, this teenage girl experienced something beautiful, yet so very painful. To protect those memories, I gently wrapped them up in a blanket and carefully hid them deep in the walls of my heart; plastering over them to conceal them and to protect them forever. Vowing to lay down my life to save them from harm ever again.

Standing at the water's edge on Dunedin causeway, the walls of my heart began to crack. During breakfast with my friend in Orlando, the walls shattered. Stepping on the plane, the walls completely collapsed. The memory I held so tightly in my heart for so many years came tumbling to the floor, crashing, and breaking into pieces. Like a little girl whose toy had just broken, letting out an earth-shattering wail, I scrambled to gather the pieces into my arms. Holding the broken pieces up to my Daddy, with tears pouring from my eyes, I cried out begging him to fix my dolly.

Are you like me? Do you have special memories or even skeletons in your closet that you keep from the light of day? Maybe they are not past experiences, but maybe they are your closet personality, ideas, and thoughts. Why do we do this? Is it because we fear the past, are ashamed of our actions, fearful of being judged, embarrassed to show our flaws, in denial if it ever happened, and insecure about our ideas and thoughts? Maybe we cannot let go after a divorce or the death of a loved one. Maybe the only reason we keep that skeleton tightly wrapped and protected in the deep crevices of our hearts is because we do not ever want to relinquish it. The grief would be more than we could ever bear.

At nineteen years old, I lost someone I loved and simultaneously faced humiliation from a group of adults I trusted. I vowed I would never let go. I vowed I would protect their memory and try to forget the humiliation I experienced, which had caused me to run. I stuffed away my emotions and pulled myself up by my bootstraps. I vowed to protect the precious memories at all costs. Letting go would risk forgetting. That could unleash the most agonizing, gut-wrenching, unimaginable grief. I could not think of anything more painful to endure.

The funny thing, holding on tight is agonizing too. Imagine holding onto a rope for dear life, tight grip, white-knuckling it to keep from drowning for thirty years. After a while, fatigue sets in, followed by sheer exhaustion. All aspects of your life are affected by this. While one hand is tightly gripping the rope, the other is trying to accomplish the tasks of everyday life with half the support. This is the trouble with holding on and refusing to let go. Eventually, you must release the grip. You cannot hold on forever. Yet, when you do, there will be pain. The grieving process will finally begin after years of deferring.

But there is hope... Jesus said, *"Come to me, all you who are weary and burdened, and I will give you rest.* Matthew 29:11 All those sleepless nights, all those bouts with emotional highs and lows, all those second guesses, all those moments of avoidance, all those nightmares, all those horrible or loving memories, all those feelings of love, joy, anticipation, hope, hate, remorse, guilt, shame, unworthiness, all that wrestling you have done over the years... He says, come to Him just as you are, lay it all at His feet and he will give you rest.

Just like so many people in the Bible experienced, Creator God is the Great Physician. He is waiting, with healing hands, to reach down to comfort and mend the hearts of his wounded beloved children. He understands the depth of our wounds. He, too, suffered every imaginable pain that we have suffered.

Somewhere in our brokenness, He meets us there to go about the work of healing. Our Daddy comes alongside, embraces us in his loving arms, picks us up, holds us tight, and then goes to work putting our broken hearts back together again.

When He is finished, He proclaims, "Look at you! You're perfect—absolutely perfect!" Then kisses us on the cheek and releases us to go play again.

Do the memories go away? No.

Will you forget? Perhaps.

Do the memories still hurt? Probably.

Can you trust God to do what He promised? Absolutely!

Do you ever feel whole again? Yes, in time.

Will you need to be reminded of His promise the next time you are faced with pain? You bet!

Can you ever trust other people again? Yes, little by little, you will learn to trust again.

Will you get hurt again? Most likely, but you will have learned the beauty of trusting the Great Physician to heal your wounds.

Questions to Ponder:

I thought about listing questions to think about, but I think it is time for you to write. Use the next three pages to write a letter to Creator Father. Tell your story of that skeleton in your closet that you have held onto for oh so long. You know the one. You have been reminded of it the whole time you read this chapter. Find a quiet place without distractions to write it out. Describe the scene, recall the initial pain, and express the emotions and memories you carry to this day. Say whatever you want to say. Creator has big shoulders. He wants to hear it. When you are done writing. Exhale. Breathe...and be still.

Let it all out…

Keep writing….

SUPERNATURAL POWER

"Don't be afraid, for I am with you.
Don't be discouraged, for I am your God.
I will strengthen you and help you.
I will hold you up with my victorious right hand."

Isaiah 41:10

I have prayed about whether to include this chapter or not. It is certainly controversial, so I want to preface these experiences by saying that while I did not need his permission, I asked my husband before I forged ahead. I was confident the Great Spirit was with me and would never leave me nor turn his back on me.

As you will recall from the previous chapters, I had already isolated and insulated myself from people outside of my practice. I had walked away from the church and begged Creator to never make me go back. I begged Him to show me what it meant to be a follower and worshiper of Jesus because what I had experienced was not what my Jesus had ever demonstrated. I was so broken and beaten down by some of His children, yet I knew this was not what He intended. I begged Him to heal my heart and bring me peace.

I asked Creator to speak to me in ways outside of what my conservative evangelical faith embraced as acceptable. I asked Creator to allow me to experience Him through His Creation in supernatural ways. For a time, I even put away my Bible, not because I didn't believe His Word to be true, but rather because I just needed to experience the power and truth of those words. His Word is hidden in my heart, so whether it is in print or not, I know enough Scripture to be reminded of His Word all day long.

Because I had removed all the barriers, I had questions for Creator and needed confirmation. I had asked Him to speak to me in radical ways. I had hit rock bottom and I needed Him to gently pick me up and hold me strong.

I received a phone call while at work one day from a friend I hadn't spoken with in a couple of years. She reached out to me because she felt worried about me and wondered what might be going on. Like I said, I had not spoken with her in a couple of years, so I knew the Spirit compelled her to call me. While we were speaking, she expressed she had just seen a vision. Because she was an Intuitive and already knew me, she wondered if I might be open to talking with one of her friends. She did not feel it was appropriate for her to work with me since she knew me.

Before the phone call...

At that time, I had been reading a book about how missionaries in the deep villages of South America experienced the supernatural power of the Great Spirit in ways we rarely ever see in North America. I wanted to experience that too!

I was also reading about how most Christians in Western civilization will never really experience the power of the Great Spirit because they don't *really* believe the Great Spirit exists. Oh, they talk about His existence and preach about His power demonstrated in Scripture, but do they *really* believe they have access to that same power? Do they *really* believe it when they see it? Or do they mock supernatural happenings and blow them off as fake? Or worse, demonic?

It was during this time that the words of the Apostle Paul rang loud and clear.

"I pray that the eyes of your heart may be enlightened so that you may know the hope to which he has called you, the riches of his glorious inheritance in his holy people, and his incomparably great power for us who believe. That Power is the same as the mighty strength he exerted when he raised Christ from the dead

and seated him at his right hand in the heavenly realms"
Ephesians 1:18 & 19.

The same power that *raised Jesus Christ from the dead* is
the same power alive in me. I have access to that power.
That changes things!

So back to the phone call.

I talked to my husband about all this, and with his
permission, decided to go speak to the Intuitive my friend
had recommended. We both prayed fervently for wisdom,
the power of the Great Spirit, and for a host of heavenly
angels to guard and protect me. I needed to hear from
Creator God, and I knew He could use anything he chose
to communicate to me.

While I was with the Intuitive, I told her I was a
Christian and that I expected God to use her to speak to
me. I would know when something she said was Truth or a
lie meant to confuse. She was so kind to oblige and
humbled to be used by Creator in such a way. She even put
away her gods and chose to call on the saints instead.

During much of our time together, she saw many
things and spoke many words, some of which resonated
with my soul. The Spirit of Discernment showed me what
was truth and what was not. The last thing she performed
was a drumming session as I lay on a table with incense
and candles burning around me.

While I was praying silently for a host of angels to
continue to watch over me from anything that may try to
confuse or interfere with what God was doing, and for the
Lord to speak clearly through this woman, I heard a door
open followed by someone entering the room. I chose to

continue to pray instead of opening my eyes to see who it might be.

While I lay on the table, the Intuitive walked a circle around the table in a counterclockwise fashion tapping her native hand drum. As she walked by my head, I could sense another person following behind her. When she had completed the circle, she stopped and asked me to sit up on the table.

She began to explain what she had been doing, what she had seen, and the words she had for me. Then she said something I will never forget, "Mindi, you are fine. You are just fine. You are surrounded by a host of angels. So many that I could hardly do anything. I felt like I was being pushed out of the room. You are one very blessed woman and have nothing to worry about!"

I remembered there had been someone else in the room, but there was no one else there. I believe an Angel from Heaven had entered the room, and His presence was felt. I also believe the host of heavenly angels I had prayed for were also there.

At that moment, I experienced the most powerful realization—Creator God's Word never fails! The same power that raised Christ from the dead was alive in me and was on full display in that room. We both knew it. We both experienced it. Creator showed up and He spoke!

You might be asking why I chose to include this experience in this book. I mean, are not Christians instructed never to entertain evil or dabble with magic or witchcraft? You are right.

"I was abandoned by the church and ostracized by the people who were supposed to support me. Instead of listening to the examples from the Bible - where the rocks cried out, Balaam's donkey spoke, and sorcerers performed miracles by calling on the name of YHWH - they turned their backs on me. The Old Testament is full of stories of those who were also rejected by their own people but found divine guidance, like the burning bush, while living amongst the Midianites."

I felt utterly crushed by the people who called themselves Christians. I did not trust anyone I knew at that time I needed to hear from Creator. I needed to experience and be reminded of His supernatural power. Nowhere was safe for me, except in the palm of His hand. As a child of the King, I knew I was safe, and He would send His angels to keep guard over me. I knew He would manifest His power and speak to my soul—through this Intuitive.

Ephesians 6:12 says, *"For our struggle is not against flesh and blood, but against the rulers, against the authorities, against the powers of this dark world and against the spiritual forces of evil in the heavenly realms."*

In our years of ministry in Ohio, I experienced this Power many times. We had fought many spiritual battles that were nothing short of angels and demons. The power of the Great Spirit and the force of Heavenly armies fought on our behalf, and we won. Our faith was strengthened by the battle.

At that moment in the Intuitive's home, I was strong and courageous in my faith, yet weak in my heart; yet I was not afraid of raging a war against the evil attacking me. I was desperate for Creator's power to be on display. He showed up and showed off! My faith was strengthened in the battle.

This was the beginning of my time in the desert where Creator would renew my strength. It started there in that room with statues, idols, tarot cards, candles, incense, and crystals. All material things that have absolutely no power unless you give them power.

It started with seeking an audible word from the Spirit through an unlikely source.

It started with feeling His Presence encircling me, watching over and protecting me.

It started with supernatural answered prayer.

It started by reminding me the battle I was facing was a war against spiritual forces, not flesh and blood.

It started with reminding me of Creator's supernatural power in my life—the same power that raised Jesus from the dead. The same power that is alive in me. The same power I have access to at any moment to do supernatural acts through me. It started with I AM —the Beginning and the End —alive in me.

After this experience, I began making regular trips to the desert to get alone and spend long periods with Creator looking for Him to show me more of His power.

While on a weekend escape, I rode around Joshua Tree National Forest on my motorcycle stopping at my favorite rock formations, including Key's View (the Lookout). Creator had already shown me during my previous visits, that if His people did not worship Him, the birds of the air, the rocks in the desert, the wind in the air, and the trees of the fields would cry out in worship to Him. I know He means that literally.

While at Key's View during sunset, I sat on a rock looking out over the Mojave Desert towards Coachella Valley. As I sat there, observing, breathing, listening, and being still in the Presence of God; the colors of the sky changed into majestic shades of orange, pink, and purple.

Suddenly, from the ravine below me, seventeen California Condors shot up into the sky like fireworks exploding. These massive birds are the largest land-flying bird in North America with a wingspan of 9.5 feet! (Ventana Wildlife Society, n.d.) From a distance they are often mistaken for turkey buzzards, however, they are larger than buzzards and boast a well-defined white triangular pattern on the underside of their wings.

These ravens began swirling in a circle and flew closer to hover over my head. I was utterly transfixed, smiling from ear to ear. I began hearing gasps and comments from everyone at the Lookout. No one understood what was happening. Some of them cautioned me to duck and cover my head for fear the condors would attack me. I had no fear whatsoever and continued to look up smiling in amazement as I watched this majestic display in the sky.

As I sat there on the rock looking up into the expanse, marveling at the swarm of ravens, Creator spoke to me. "My child, this is my power. I control the heavens and the earth and all that is in it. This same power is alive in you. All the power of heaven and earth is at your disposal. All the things I did when I walked this earth, you can do more and greater than that. You are my child, and I am with you. Speak and it will be done." At that moment, I told the ravens they could leave. Immediately they flew off!

Creator God's word never fails!

I hopped on my motorcycle, which I had already named "Raven", and headed to another location inside the park. This path is for off-roading vehicles, so I did not go far on my cruiser. I stood along the path looking up into the sky, crying out to God. "I cannot stay in California. I cannot take it anymore. Please show me where to go!"

Just then another condor began calling from a distance. I recognized this bird as my friend who lived in the cleft of the rocks high above the formation named Split Rock.

Upon arrival, during all my trips to Joshua Tree, I would make my way to Split Rock to spend time journaling. Just minutes later, this beautiful condor would fly down from his perch atop the mountain of rocks to sit on a boulder near me. It was like he had been waiting for my return so we could visit together.

He would sit on the rock staring at me. I would look at him and marvel at his beauty while also asking Creator to speak through him to me. On many occasions, our spirits connected and spoke to each other. In those moments, the peace I felt was unmatched by anything else I had ever experienced. I was experiencing God!

I had removed all the barriers that say, "This is how God speaks today." I told Creator I wanted Him to have complete freedom to speak to me however He chose.

On this occasion, the condor flew across the desert towards me, calling to me. As he flew past, I sensed he was calling me to follow in the direction he was traveling. He continued to call until he disappeared in the distance. When I got back to my cottage, I looked up the direction he had come from and was flying towards.

Out in the desert, it is very easy to get turned around and lose all sense of direction. What I discovered was he was flying in a southeasterly direction. I believe this was a message from Creator. I believe he used this raven to show me the way to go.

Some will argue these experiences were not God, saying this was my imagination or possibly even demonic activity. I can assure you, I have come face to face with demons over the years. None of this was demonic, but rather Creator God demonstrating his enormous power.

Remember, I had removed the human barriers defining how He speaks to people living in America as being vastly different than how He speaks to people in other places around the world. I had told Creator he had free reign with me. If He could appear to Moses as a burning bush in the middle of the desert, or cause a donkey to speak to Balaam in the Old Testament, BC then He could speak to me through an Intuitive or a condor in the middle of the California desert in 2019 AD.

As I reflect on this experience and all the supernatural ways God moved, I am reminded of how important it is for me to continue to set aside time every day to spend watching, praying, meditating, and waiting for God to speak. I must be honest. I have never been very good at morning devotions. While this practice is certainly beneficial and creates good habits, I have found it to be something to check off my to-do list every day. This is another practice that I believe we have created in our Christian culture that is not "biblical" but simply cultural.

Do not get me wrong! I do not mean that reading and studying the Bible is wrong. Far from it! I think our culture has dictated a practice that is expected to be done in such a manner and when not achieved is frowned upon.

Think of it this way: If you were told the best way to know your spouse is to spend time reading a letter he wrote to you, and talking to him every single morning for thirty minutes, would you think that a little odd? Like that is it? Spend thirty minutes a day with your spouse and your marriage will grow and become rock solid. Really?

What Creator has called us to is a relationship with Him. He wants more from us than thirty minutes every day. He wants all of us. He wants us to spend time with him, love him, walk with him, talk with him, listen to him, cry with him, share with him all of life's stuff. Jesus calls us His bride, not his student. He calls us his child, not his pet.

He calls us pure and holy, not judged and unworthy. He wants more from us than to check off time spent with Him on our to-do list.

The Scripture says to *"pray without ceasing"* 1 Thessalonians 5:17. That means to constantly be talking and listening to God all day long as we go about our lives. Staying in tune with the prompting of the Spirit requires this. How else would we recognize his promptings? *"The sheep hear the shepherd's voice and respond"* John 10:27.

We too can do the same by building this kind of relationship with Creator. Then when you decide to spend time reading His word it is out of a desire to learn more about Him, not because you were told this is the only way to grow in your faith.

Can you imagine the freedom you would experience in your faith journey if you literally tore down all the barriers that you have erected that are cultural expectations, and instead lived only by Biblical expectations?

Can you imagine what it would be like to just sit quietly listening and observing—just waiting for Creator God to come near and speak to you?

Can you imagine what it would be like if He spoke to you through His Creation? How different would you be?

Questions to Ponder:

At what point in your life have you been desperate to hear from Creator God?

Did you expect He would show up?

How radical is your faith? Are you willing to trust Him to do the impossible?

How do you feel about these experiences discussed in this chapter?

In what ways do you find them too radical? In what ways do you find them inspiring?

Do you believe He can speak to you in supernatural ways too?

Are you willing to remove the barriers to give Him free reign?

Is your soul awakening?

STILL SMALL VOICE

"Have you ever heard the earth breathe?"

—Kate Chopin

It is not often you hear of people going to the desert to find life. Usually, the desert claims life. I was already mentally, emotionally, and spiritually dead. So, the desert could either claim me or breathe new life into me. Either way, I was going to the desert.

These trips reminded me of the story of Elijah in 1 Kings 19:1-3 when he learns that Jezebel was going to kill him out of revenge for the death of the prophets of Baal on Mount Carmel. So, Elijah fled out into the desert to run for his life. He found a broom tree laid down under the shade of the bush and prayed for his death. As he fell asleep, an angel of the Lord brought him water and food two times. Creator God allowed Elijah to rest under the broom tree, giving him strength to continue his journey to Mount Horeb.

This story is beautifully told in Felix Mendelssohn's oratorio *"Elijah"*. When Elijah lays down, he cries out to God in the aria "It is Enough, Oh Lord, Now Take Away My Life":

"It is enough; O Lord, now take my life for I am not better than my fathers! I desire to live no longer: now let me die, for my days are but vanity! I have been very jealous for the Lord God of Hosts! For the children of Israel have broken Thy covenant, and thrown down thine altars and slain all Thy prophets —slain them with the sword: and I, even I, only am left; and they seek my life to take it away" Job 7:16; I Kings 19: 4,10.

The angel of the Lord appears to Elijah the second time while he sleeps singing *"O Rest in the Lord"*:

"O rest in the Lord; wait patiently for Him, then He shall give thee thy heart's desires. Commit thy way unto Him, and trust in Him, and fret not thyself because of evil doers" Psalm 37: 1, 4, 7.

Strengthened by the food provided to him by the angel, Elijah traveled forty days and forty nights to escape to Mount Horeb where he slept in a cave. While he was sleeping, the Creator came to him and asked him what he was doing. Elijah explained how he had worked so zealously for Him, yet the Israelites refused to worship Him, killed all the other prophets, and now want to kill him too. Creator told Elijah to go stand out on the mountain in the presence of Creator where the glory of Creator was about to pass by. So, Elijah did as he was instructed. In the oratorio, the chorus breaks forth singing "Behold, God the Lord, Passeth By":

"Behold! God the Lord passed by! And a mighty wind rent the mountains around, broke in pieces the rocks, broke them before the Lord: but yet the Lord was not in the tempest. Behold! God the Lord passed by! And the sea was upheaved, and the earth was shaken, but yet the Lord was not in the earthquake. And after the earthquake there came a fire: but yet the Lord was not in the fire. And after the fire, there came a still small voice and in that still voice, onward came the Lord" (I Kings 19:11, 12).

The story of Elijah resonates with me. I certainly do not claim to be a prophet; but I feel his heartache, exhaustion, and fear in service to the King of Kings here on this earth. If I can recall, I would estimate the time I spent in the desert to be about forty days and nights.

That moment the ravens shot up out of the ravine, reminds me of how Creator God appeared to Elijah on Mount Horeb and the display of power He paraded in front of Elijah, yet God was not in any of it. He was in the still small voice. Creator spoke to me in a still small voice —just like He speaks to you too. He is not loud and abrasive. He is not rude and demanding. He is meek and gentle. He does not demand to be heard. He waits patiently for us to listen.

The times I spent in the desert were spiritually rich for me. Creator God showed himself in many ways. The majesty of the ginormous rock formations, the glory in the most beautiful sunsets sprawling across the desert, the valley below the mountaintop view, the beauty of the tiniest of insects to the largest of birds, the cold breeze at night and fierce desert sun by day, the millions of stars, and beautiful bright white moon illuminating the deep blue night sky. God created it all and His glory shines all around us, but His power is in the still small voice.

During times of deep grief and anguish, He protects our weary souls. He protected Elijah under the shadow of the broom tree and sent angels to feed him. He protected me under the shadow of a massive azalea shrub at the cottage where I stayed on my trips to the desert. He gave me food and water to quench my soul. He displayed his power and showed me that I have access to this kind of power too. Yet, He spoke to me in a still small voice.

I trusted Him to show himself. I trusted Him to heal my soul. I trusted Him to protect me on my journey. I trusted Him to provide for me in the desert. I trusted Him to speak.

...and He did.

The more time I take to spend in silence, the more I hear Him speak to me—the more you'll hear Him speak to you too. *This is the way; walk in it* Isaiah 30:21.

Questions to Ponder:

I want you to stop for a minute and dream with me. Be honest with yourself. Even if you are perfectly happy with your life as it is right now, there are probably some things you would like to learn, try, or explore. There are probably goals you have considered achieving. I would imagine there are even things about your life today that are not "ideal" or not what you planned. I want you to take a minute and do the following exercise.

Draw a picture of what your ideal life looks like. Even if your drawing looks like chicken scratch and stick figures; draw a picture using images, and single-word descriptors, and include symbols and colors that have special meaning to you.

When you are done, post this picture above your computer or somewhere you will see it daily. Creator Father says He will give you the desires of your heart. If your heart and His heart are in alignment, His desires and your desires will come into alignment. He promises to fulfill those dreams and desires.

Is your soul awakening?

TRUST

"Trust in the Lord with all your heart;
don't lean on your own understanding.
In all your ways acknowledge Him
and He will direct your paths."

Proverbs 3:5-6

Trust.

That is a big word, is it not? We can give it and we can receive it. We can gain it and we can lose it. We can choose to be trustworthy, or we can choose to be deceitful. One thing is certain, it is a choice.

Our brains make millions of decisions every single day. And every single day, we must decide to offer up trust or take a leap and give trust. Sometimes we have been hurt by a situation in the past, so it makes trusting again in a similar situation very difficult. Yet, we still get to choose to trust.

Sometimes we have been the ones to offend in the past. In our attempts to do over, we need to be trusted to overcome and be successful. Perhaps our wealth of knowledge gets in the way of the process because we know too much and just need to trust the outcome even when it does not make sense. Do you think our brains have trust issues? Not too long ago a wise man said,

"Trust in the LORD with all your heart; don't lean on your own understanding. In all your ways, acknowledge Him and He will direct your paths" Proverbs 3:5-6.

The word trust and multiple variations of the word are used 351 times in the Bible. I would say trusting is difficult for our brains, hence the reason God knew we would need to be reminded of this every single day of the year.

Growing up as a pastor's kid and then becoming a pastor's wife, I have had my fair share of hurt over the nearly five decades of full-time Christian ministry. "Church hurt" is a cliche being tossed around as a description of the pain people experience in their local churches. I guess it is comforting to know I am not alone. But WOW! How can this be? How can it be that other

Christians are inflicting so much pain that we now have a readily known title for it?

Remember that condor and the direction it was flying —southeasterly? Well, God moved us in a southeasterly direction just *three months* later. Six weeks after we moved to eastern North Carolina, Covid lockdowns began.

Here we were, living in an apartment in the middle of North Raleigh, where we knew no one, other than the patients I had met at work. My husband worked from home and my youngest daughter was working with an online charter school to finish out her last year of high school.

When we first moved to Raleigh, we visited a few churches. We found one we liked, but that very week, the lockdowns began. No churches were allowed to meet, so everything went to online services. I must admit, while we were disappointed, I was relieved. I had just come off a long stint of emotional upheaval all centered around a lifetime of church hurt. The last thing I was ready to do was enter into a new church to face the very real prospect of more "church hurt." So yeah, for me, I was rejoicing! Creator heard my cry of anguish and fear and forced the whole world into lockdown. *(commence sinister laughing)*

While I am only teasing about sinister laughing, I was rejoicing. I did not have to feel guilty for not going to church. I did not have to step out there and make myself vulnerable. I did not have to pretend that everything was ok, and I was a happy Christian woman and pastor's wife living a wonderfully blessed life. Deep inside, I was anything but.

On the weekends, my husband and I would take off on our motorcycles and ride hundreds of miles exploring North Carolina and the Blue Ridge Mountains of Virginia.

We would leave as soon as I got out of work on Friday and head to the hills only to return late Sunday afternoon in time to get ready to go back to work. We lived for the weekends—to ride!

About six months into apartment life during a pandemic, we had explored so much of North Carolina on our motorcycles, that we knew it like the backs of our hands. I was also restless about buying a house. Something in me told me we had to buy a home and we had to move fast. My husband wondered why I was in such a hurry. He was perfectly content with apartment life but did not hold me back. He knows this about me. If something is burning in me to get done, he steps back and lets me do it. There is usually an underlying important reason I am passionate about it, even if I do not know what that reason could be.

A couple of months later, we found our home in a little rural town called Selma, NC— "The Crossroads of Innovation and Tradition." As soon as we closed on our home, the housing market exploded! We then understood why I had the sense we had to buy a house before the end of 2020.

Several months later, my daughter, a recent graduate and chiropractor by then, and her husband moved to Selma and opened our chiropractic practice in town. Selma did not have any healthcare. The practice took off like wildfire.

My daughter had started to attend a church in another nearby town. She was so thrilled with this church, that she begged my husband and I to visit and see for ourselves. She sent me a recording of a Sunday evening worship event the church had done. I was so impressed with the music, that I decided to step out and tiptoe to church the next Sunday. The church, the pastors, the people, the music blew me away and blessed my socks off. As a trained opera singer, it is always hard for me to fit into contemporary church music cultures, but there was hope for me at this church. After the service, my daughter introduced us to the music pastor, making sure to inform him I could sing, even though I was not ready to reveal that. He was thrilled and immediately invited me to join the choir.

Now when I say church choir, you might be inclined to roll your eyes and reminisce of grandma's church choir. I can assure you, this is not the kind of choir I was being invited to join. The Princeton Church in Princeton, NC has one of the most top-notch church choirs I've heard in a very long time. If you are familiar with the Brooklyn Tabernacle Choir, this is the style of choir music they sing. They are just as good too!

Before we left that Sunday, the music pastor gave me a copy of the recent album they professionally recorded. I thought to myself, "Wow! How could a choir with this caliber of music exist in the middle of pig and tobacco farms in rural, NC?" It took me a few months, but I decided to join the choir and give the church a chance. We have been attending there ever since.

In January of 2022, I contracted a severe case of Covid, and resigned from my chiropractic job in Raleigh, followed by a year of intense long-haul Covid. Most of 2022 was spent laying on the couch or my bed with crippling pain over my entire body. After months of functional neurology to rehab my brain, I was able to walk again. After chiropractic adjustments every week and intense functional nutrition work, I was able to do more and more. I spent that year meditating for hours, praying, being still, and listening to God's still small voice; a year later, I was finally out from under it all.

During this time, I physically could not attend church and the church knew I was so very sick. Do you know what? I received numerous cards, phone calls, texts, and social media messages from choir members checking in on me and letting me know they were praying for me. This was such a blessing to me.

I had not experienced anything like this in recent years of ministry. I was always the one offering care and concern, but rarely was it reciprocated. My daughter reported back to me almost weekly with words of encouragement and prayers sent to me from people she had spoken to at church each Sunday.

Once I had mostly recovered, she commented that people still asked about me and that I should consider coming back to church soon. Immediately, my defenses went up. I responded, "Why are they asking about me? They hardly even know me!" Man, those walls of fear are so thick!

But then...

I was treating a patient who attends our church. She asked me which of the three services I attend. *(deep inhale)* I responded with, "Do you have a minute? I have a break in my schedule, and this could take a little bit to explain." Before I knew it, the fire hose was unleashed. I am not sure what I was thinking. I am not sure what was going through her mind either. Perhaps, "Why on earth did I ask?" But she was so kind as to let me vent my struggle.

When the conversation was over and she had left the office, I realized something. The reason I was so afraid to go to church was because I did not think I could trust Princeton Church, or any church for that matter. Years of heartache had broken my spirit and trust.

Despite all the times I had been hurt, I realized something while I was standing there talking to my patient. The lead pastor, his wife, the music pastor, and the people of Princeton Church had given me absolutely no reason to NOT trust them. I had thrown out multiple curve balls that year to test the reaction I would get.

Will they judge me?

Will I be labeled?

Will they think I am a bad Christian?

Will they treat me like I am an outsider because I am not from here?

Can I sing in this choir even though I have a projecting operatic voice?

Will I be ridiculed for talking too loudly, being too dramatic and expressive?

Am I allowed to be part of the motorcycle riders' small group because I am not a guy?

Will the women of the church think I am nothing like them and shun me?

Will they think my style of worship outside the church walls complete with meditation, dreams, visions, incense, and communing with nature is inappropriate for an evangelical Christian?

Can I speak freely about my radical faith and not get shut down?

Can I be a female, medical professional, and yet a biker chic at the same time without feeling judged or shunned?

Can I be me—ALL OF ME—and not have to protect parts of me and become someone entirely different to be accepted—like I have done since I was a young teenager, deeply wounded?

You see, wherever the voices in my head were coming from the fear of continued pain and rejection was oh-so very real. Standing in my office and spewing my struggle, the Lord opened my heart to show me not one time—not one single time—had I felt unaccepted, judged, unwelcomed, or cast aside at Princeton Church. Not one single time was I expected to be someone I was not. Not one single time had I felt who God created me to be was unacceptable to them.

I had felt incredibly welcomed and loved. Princeton Church was offering me *their* trust because they trusted me. Yet I did not see that I could trust Creator God and this amazing church until that simple innocent question was asked of me, "Which service do you attend?"

… and then the walls came tumbling down.

Questions to Ponder:

How has your spirit or trust been broken?

How deep did that wound go?

Do you recognize the impact it has on the relationships you form or do not form?

If you can imagine how different your life would be if you were able to trust certain relationships knowing that you still may get hurt, would you allow your walls to topple?

Do you think Creator Father is trying to help you learn you can trust Him?

Does trusting God scare you?

What is one simple baby step you could take to test God's trust in a particular situation you are facing?

Which service do you attend?

Is your soul awakening?

PROTECTION

*"For I know the plans I have for you;
plans to prosper you and not to harm you,
plans to give you hope and a future."*

Jeremiah 29:11

I was reading through the last several years of my journals just before the New Year of 2022. If you will recall, in January 2022, I became very sick. I came across this entry, which had been written just 4 weeks prior:

December 29, 2021

"Do not be conformed to the pattern of this world, but be transformed by the renewing of your mind. Then you will be able to test and approve what God's will is—his good, pleasing, and perfect will" Romans 12:2.

As I meditated on this verse throughout the past year (2021), I noticed my perspective and attitude toward many things were changing. 2021 was yet another challenging year for me. I had many things on my plate that took a lot of my time and physical/mental energy. At one point, I felt I was nearing burnout and worried I would not be able to keep going.

However, the Lord was gracious and gave me lots of weekend motorcycle runs to get out of town and catch my breath. He blessed me with the finances to begin doing some of the home improvements I had on my list since buying my house. He gave me my voice back which is probably the most thrilling blessing I have ever received. And the icing on the cake was he miraculously gave me a little bit of artistic talent to start painting. Motorcycle riding, home improvements, singing, and painting—all the things I love that also help me to decompress, reflect and express myself.

I certainly had moments of bad attitudes and not great perspectives, but by the end of 2021, I can say I noticed significant improvement. The truth is the more I recognized I needed to turn things around and not get sucked into the garbage of this world, the easier it was to stay on track and the happier I became. I can quite literally say, I transformed my mind by changing the way I think! God's Word is true and never fails!

As I moved into 2022, I asked God to reveal the verse He'd have me focus my attention on. Wouldn't you know it? He gave me two. Several years ago, He did this, and it was hands down the hardest year of my life! On one hand, I was stepping into 2022 with fear and trepidation, and on the other, I was reminded of 2021's verse to change the way I think as I set my focus on next year's Scripture passages:

"For I know the plans I have for you; plans to prosper you and not to harm you, plans to give you hope and a future." Jeremiah 29:11

"The Lord bless you & keep you; the Lord make his face to shine upon you and be gracious to you; the Lord turn his face toward you and give you peace." Numbers 6:24-26

Throughout 2021, the Lord has been showing me these verses repeatedly through a dear 83-year-old friend who has become such a sweet blessing in my life, and through my pastor who speaks this blessing over us each Sunday. It's now the end of December 2021, and it was not till this week, that God told me THESE are the verses I have for you next year (the verses above). And you know what? He not only gave me these verses, but He gave me two very important trusted people in my life to remind me of these verses regularly. He gave me His Word and He has surrounded me with Godly support too. I am blessed and grateful.

The words that summarize these verses are Trust & Protection

The image in my mind is that of a weeping willow tree next to a private pond with a beautiful white trumpeter swan floating on the water—so I painted it to frame and keep

*on my desk at work to remind me daily of God's plan for me
this year.*

It was a long drive home that fateful day in January
2022, just 4 weeks after that journal entry. Shaking from
head to toe, with burning pain that began in my lower
back and coursing through my legs like an electrical
current, I prayed for safety and protection to get home in
one piece. An hour later, I nearly crawled into the house,
dropping everything at the door, and headed straight to
bed. My husband had never seen me like this before. As
my fever spiked and the burning pain started to spread up
my spine to my brain, I began to pray for The Great
Physician to guard my body and heal me quickly.

My family had all been sick with COVID-19 long
before me but bounced back quickly without residual
symptoms. I was doing all the right things to stay healthy
by eating an anti-inflammatory diet, taking the
recommended supplements, and getting plenty of rest.
Two years of exposure and I was doing just fine... until
that day.

As I wrote in my journal entry just weeks prior, I was
teetering on the brink of burnout. I had jumped from an
emotional few years of processing past hurt and loss,
feeling incredibly lonely and unaccepted, to starting a new
job at a chiropractic office the day after arriving in North
Carolina—the moving truck had not even arrived yet!

Things got off to a bumpy start at my new job too. The
staff and I did not get along too well. No matter how hard
I tried and however many conversations I had with my
boss, the staff saw me as no more than another staff
member and not as a doctor. To make matters worse,
Covid struck just six weeks after touching down in North

Carolina. Being a healthcare worker during COVID had its challenges which compounded the others.

One year later, my boss took an extended leave of absence to care for a personal matter. I gladly stepped up to the plate to take over the entire practice for several months in his absence. However, after several months, I could feel my body fading. Brain fog, memory loss, stumbling speech, body aches and pains, loss of sleep, and terrible headaches all began to hit me.

When he returned to practice, I continued with the care with most of the patient base. A few months later, there did not seem to be an end in sight. I would leave for work in the dark and return home in the dark, rarely seeing the light of day. Work, eat, sleep, repeat was the story of my life. I only saw my husband on the weekends but was too tired to do much of anything at all.

My boss had already begun discussing my contract renewal for the next two years and was pressuring me for an answer. I had been praying for Creator to make His Will known for me in this situation. I loved my patients, and I loved chiropractic. The pay was great. I even enjoyed the commute. Relations with the staff still were an issue, with the disrespect trickling into how they related to my patients too.

My husband and I had discussed how we could use the income for a couple more years while he was growing his consulting business. Feeling like the Great Spirit had made it clear, I renewed my contract and began to work on changing my mindset. If this was what the Spirit wanted of me, then I needed to gain a better attitude and outlook.

The day I told my husband I renewed my contract, he was shocked! He did not want to see me drag on for another two years. Unfortunately, it was too late. I am a woman of my word, so I started to pray for the Creator to give me the strength, stamina, energy, and physical health to press on for two more years. I prayed for Him to quickly help me transform my mind by changing the way I think.

Christmas came with much relief! That one week a year of vacation was glorious! After family festivities were over, my husband and I took a much-needed road trip to Williamsburg, VA to celebrate our anniversary.

While still quite tired, January 2nd came, and it was time to go back to work. Within two days, I felt like I was right back where I had ended in 2021 before vacation. Nothing had changed and I was discouraged, but I kept reminding myself to transform my mind by changing the way I think.

The second week, my boss called to inform the office staff he had COVID-19, and that we all should get tested. Still negative, I plugged away carrying the load of the entire practice again. Two weeks later while treating patients, my low back began to hurt. Except it felt different than the low back pain I had been experiencing off and on that year. By the end of the morning shift, I was checking my temperature, because I felt so off. Yet, no fever. I chalked it up to fatigue.

During lunch, I laid down on a therapy table and put ice on my back. After lunch, I felt a little better and got back to work. Within an hour, deep aching pain began to move down the back of my legs. I started to feel weak, but I still had four more hours and a full caseload of patients to treat. However, just one hour later, my legs were burning like fire and the pain in my lower back was unbearable. I could barely hold myself up. I looked at the schedule and saw that a young family with a newborn was about to walk in the door. I made the call. I did not know what was wrong with me, but if it was Covid, we had to close the practice before exposing the family.

I stopped to get tested on my way home. Shaking, aching, burning, and incredibly weak, I drove the hour-long commute praying I would make it. By the time I got home, the fever kicked in, spiking to 104F. I did not know if my test was positive or not, I knew this had to be COVID-19 and I was very sick.

For six long weeks, I battled every possible symptom you can imagine. What became apparent was I might not survive it. I was not scared but I surely did not want to end up like some of my extended family who did not survive. That year, we lost fourteen family members to Covid. They all died in the hospital, alone. There was no way I was going to do that to my family or myself for that matter.

I will never forget the raw conversation I had with my husband. While I was coherent, I made my wishes known. The look in his eyes was something I will never forget. The fear he must have been experiencing was awful. He never left my side and was ever so vigilant day and night.

At one point, my daughters were at my home checking on me. They were about to leave. We were standing in the kitchen talking when suddenly, I grabbed my chest and wailed. Searing pain shot through my heart. Immediately, my oldest daughter (the doctor) went to work. Within a couple of minutes, the pain was gone, and I was fine. The vitals were good. Was it a trans-ischemic attack, angina, or even a heart attack? Regardless, I refused to go to the hospital. I was fine now. Please note: I advise seeking emergency medical care. However, under the circumstances of the times, I did not trust the medical care I would get. What can I say? Doctors make the worst patients.

Six weeks later, I was still battling a low-grade fever. With the growing list of now fifty-plus symptoms, and the never-ending text messages coming in daily from my boss asking how I was feeling and when I would be returning, I decided to attempt to resume working. My follow-up test was negative. So, I felt the pressure to return, though I was in no shape to be seeing patients.

That Monday, I braved the drive to the office. By the time I arrived, I could hardly walk. My blood pressure was spiking, as was my heart rate. I was weak and unable to catch my breath—just from driving. That week, my symptoms grew worse in intensity. The weekend came and I crashed hard. The fever spiked and I was bedridden the entire weekend.

On Monday, I returned to work again, barely able to stand up. Patients were worried and kept asking why I was even there. That day, I called to make an appointment with a functional neurologist. I knew that my brain was under attack and that modern medicine didn't have answers for Covid induced "Dysautonomia" (the endless set of symptoms I was experiencing).

After my exam, my functional neurologist was stunned and gave me orders to stop working immediately or I was not going to make it. She also informed me my healing process would take at least six months and that I needed to plan accordingly. That was it. The Spirit spoke loudly and this time. I guess His still small voice had not been getting through.

I wrote my letter of resignation, submitted it that Friday effective immediately, and commenced with a year of intense therapy to recover. I knew all that was happening was Creator God's plan, but it did not go over well with my boss. I resolved in my mind to quietly accept the situation and move on. I cannot control other people's reactions. I can only control mine.

"Do not be conformed to the pattern of this world but be transformed by the renewing of your mind. Then you will be able to test and approve what God's will is—his good, pleasing, and perfect will" Romans 12:2.

Those weeks and many months to follow were discouraging yet bathed in peace. It is so hard to describe how things sat in my soul. I mean here I was disabled, out of work, bed-ridden, fighting for my life—yet, at peace. The Spirit washed over me during those long months and began to teach me more and more about His Power and all He has in store for me. He gave me peace that I was going to make it and would thrive. Yet, I needed time for Him to do a massive work of restoration in my life—physically, mentally, emotionally, and spiritually.

I would not change that entire year of healing for anything. The lessons I learned and the wisdom I gained are incalculable! My soul was awakening!

Questions to Ponder:

Have you ever experienced a hardship that upended your entire life?

How did you process that?

It is so much easier to get angry, scared, and irrational. However, have you ever faced hardship by completely laying it at the feet of Jesus?

How did it change you?

What lessons did you learn?

Do you find it easier now to stay calm and hand it over to God when faced with trials and troubles?

If you have never experienced this, the next time a trial presents itself, stop and take a deep breath. As you exhale, ask Creator to do what it is He desires. Ask Him to give you peace during the storm. Then put that on repeat like a broken record. Eventually, you will find it becomes easier to do.

Is your soul awakening?

FAITH

"The Lord bless you & keep you;
the Lord make his face to shine upon you
and be gracious to you;
the Lord turn his face toward you
and give you peace."

Numbers 6:24-26

All of us experienced COVID-19—even if we did not get sick yourself, you experienced it. Illness, long-haul symptoms, boredom, isolation, depression, anxiety, loneliness, job loss, financial distress, homeschooling, lack of childcare, never-ending online meetings, increased hours working, grocery and meal deliveries, the endless stream of delivery trucks knocking at our doors, abuse in all its forms, addiction in all its forms, and most profoundly, the loss of loved ones and friends. Those nearly three years of massive changes in all our lives took its toll on the little corners of our homes and the world at large.

Strikingly, we saw immense positive changes too. Because everything controlled by humans was limited, we saw the earth rest and reproduce new life, even some species of animals that were in the danger zone of extinction repopulated and are no longer in danger. Many babies were conceived during that time. After I returned to practice, I had the pleasure of seeing many of them born. Home improvement projects, and of course the housing market, surged to unprecedented demand. People across the globe discovered they could fend for themselves by practicing a variety of homesteading skills—gardening, making homemade foods, raising small farm animals for their eggs, dairy, soap, lotions, cleaning supplies, and the like.

Gas prices soared. Grocery prices skyrocketed. Grocery store shelves were empty. Scientific evidence was misconstrued and incomplete yet broadcast as absolute fact. Our leaders lied or at least misspoke all too often. Trust in our leadership and medical professionals eroded. Free speech was severely limited.

Churches closed. Businesses closed. Jobs were lost. Government crackdowns began in response to survival techniques implemented. Some communities prohibited or restricted small farming. Some threatened home gardening. The selling of homestead animals and garden produce was further limited. Yet, the people continued to find a way to provide for themselves and their families. For many, they continue to do so because they realize the rewards.

After the lockdowns lifted, we saw many big box businesses close for good. Mid-paying jobs were limited, though low-paying jobs could not find enough employees. Some churches saw record growth, while many churches recorded low attendance or closed entirely. Some of the worst natural disasters occurred around the globe—fires, earthquakes, floods, volcanic eruptions, and so on.

Gun violence and terrorism were in the news daily. Methamphetamine and Fentanyl addictions and overdoses were exploding around the globe. Pure evil was paraded and celebrated across daytime television as morally and ethically good. Schools and social norms were eroding at a frightful pace. Social media became a cesspool of evil, narcissism, violence, and underground sinister activity. It seemed our world had gone utterly mad!

Why did all this happen?

Why are so many people facing financial crises that were stable before?

Why were we lied to by the people we thought we could trust?

Why did so many people have to die?

Why is evil seen as good?

Why is the world a very different place today than it was just five years ago?

Why is God allowing all this? Does He even care?

How could a good God allow such evil things to happen?

Where is God?

Is there even a God?

When churches resumed their gatherings, God brought people to our church that otherwise may never have gone to church. The congregation has grown exponentially ever since.

Being relatively new to the church, I did not know how long this tradition had been going on. At the close of every sermon, one of the pastors prayed over the congregation with this blessing:

"The Lord bless you & keep you; the Lord make his face to shine upon you and be gracious to you; the Lord turn his face toward you and give you peace" Numbers 6:24-26.

The first several times I heard this, I didn't think much of it. Maybe I zoned out during the closing prayer? Who knows, but after a few weeks, the prayer of blessing over the congregation struck me profoundly. I realized it was one of the verses God gave me to meditate on that year!

This passage is called "The Priestly Benediction" or the "Aaronic Blessing" by theologians today. When I was researching theological discussions around this passage, I discovered there is much to be said about this passage. I am going to keep this simple. If you would like to dig deeper, please do! For the sake of this context, I am just going to describe the essence or maybe a more fitting word is the "fragrance" of the keywords in this passage.

Each line in this three-line blessing is a call for God's *movement* on the person followed by His *activity* on their behalf. The request becomes incrementally stronger with each line of blessings on the individual, starting with a trickle and leading to an outpouring.

> *The Lord bless you & keep you;*

> *The Lord make his face to shine upon you and be gracious to you;*

> *The Lord turn his face toward you and give you peace.*

<u>Lord</u>: *Yahweh* (YHWH) - The word *Yahweh* comes from the Hebrew word "I am." It is translated as "the LORD." He brings into existence whatever exists. He is the self-existent eternal God. In Hebrew, the word *Yahweh* is considered the holiest of names for the Lord. In fact, so holy, Jews are forbidden to speak the holy name, because they believe the perfect most holy name of God cannot be spoken by an imperfect and unholy man. In prayers they use *Adonai* (My Lord) and in conversation *HaShem* (The Name).

Christians, however, believe that the atoning blood of Jesus Christ on the cross washed us clean. Standing before Him perfect and holy, we can enter the presence of the Lord and speak directly to Him using the name *Yahweh* because He sees us as pure and righteous.

<u>You</u>: the word "you" is used in this prayer about a specific person or a small body of people, rather than a collective group of people at large. Aaron (a priest) spoke this prayer of blessing over his sons (priests of the tribes of Judah) specifically. He did not pray this over the entire nation of Judah, but rather over the leaders of Judah.

Today, this prayer is used similarly—as a prayer over a specific body of people. My pastors pray this prayer over the congregation every week—not over the entire nation of Christians in all of America or the world. Rather they pray this prayer of blessing over those they have been charged to lead.

Reminder, God declared as priests those who have accepted Christ's atonement on the cross as salvation for our sins. So, if that is you, you too can pray this prayer of blessing as a benediction to other priests. You do not need to be an ordained pastor or elder to pray this blessing over others. "...*for you are a chosen people. You are royal priests, a holy nation, God's very own possession*" 1 Peter 2:9.

Bless: the word "bless" in this passage means to empower, to make productive, and even to cause to prosper. It is not a feeling or sentiment, as we typically use the word today. God blessed a barren couple Abraham and Sarah with a son, Isaac. God gave Jacob & Esau—a lifetime of progeny and acquisition of goods. A blessing is one of the benefits received both tangibly as well as intangibly.

Keep: the word "keep" is used to describe how a gardener would plant and tend to a garden or how a shepherd would watch over, pay careful attention to, and protect his flock. *Yahweh* is often referred to as a shepherd who guards his flock by keeping watch over them (paying close attention), protecting them from harm.

Make His face to shine upon you: this phrase is used to emphasize God's *emotion*—that of joy and a benevolent attitude towards his worshipers. His eyes would be lit up with pride and joy. Think of Him having a sparkle in his eyes, smiling from ear to ear, expressing favor and contentment as if to say, "That's *my* kid!"

Be gracious: "to show grace" is used to describe a disposition of kindness. We all have met someone who is genuinely a kind person—it's just their natural disposition.

They wouldn't hurt a fly. A kind disposition is what the word "grace" is referring to in this passage.

Lift up His countenance upon you (turn his face towards you): in contrast to "make his face shine upon you" this phrase is not an emotion. Rather it is used to describe an *attitude* exuding readiness to help—like someone always ready to step in when needed to pick up the slack, helping to get a job done, never complaining. It's in God's nature to be a helper.

Give you peace: the most basic meaning is for well-being, wholeness, and completeness. (Martens, Fall 2009; Vol.38. No.2.)

To summarize this passage or maybe to word it a little more descriptively in today's language, I would suggest it could go something like this:

"May the most holy Creator Father, give you (insert your name) what you desire in tangible and intangible ways, and guard over you, protecting you all the days of your life.

May the Creator of the entire universe, with a sparkle in his eyes, beaming from ear to ear, exuding pride for you (insert your name), be ever so kind to you.

May the most holy Creator God, step in and help you (insert your name) accomplish all your tasks from day to day, even the things you only dream about doing, and when you have accomplished these things, give you a sense of completeness, wholeness, and true well-being."

Can you just picture Him? The God of the Universe, Creator God, who has existed from the beginning of all time. Jehovah, *Yahweh* kneeling in front of you in a posture of pure kindness, smiling at you with a radiant wide-mouth, teeth gleaming smile, almost laughing from the amount of joy and pride in his heart He has for you? Can you envision Him watching over you, protecting you from harm, blessing you beyond all you can imagine or hope, in ways you cannot always see, reaching out His hand to help you do the things you must, even accomplishing the impossible dreams?

I picture a little girl in the garden picking flowers. Creator walks over to her, kneels ever so sweetly, smiling like a proud Daddy, and then reaches out to help her pick more flowers and place them in her basket. When they are done, the little girl giggles with gratitude and skips away with the pretty basket of flowers to present to her mommy. While her Daddy stands up dusting off his knees, watching her deliver this blessing to his beautiful bride. What pride, what joy, what contentment, what favor the father must exude!

Is there a God? Does he care? I believe so. This same God allows mankind to decide for themselves. He gives them the freedom to accept Him or to deny Him. In that acceptance, we inherit his favor (blessing). In denying Him, though, the inheritance is withheld.

I choose to believe that this is the Creator God I serve. Even though there is trouble and sorrow all around me, my Father in Heaven loves me. He wants what is best for me. I may not see the future, but He does. He only does what is good. He takes what I see as bad and works it for my good. I trust His plan.

Questions to Ponder:

No question this time... just go back and read the original passage, then reread my paraphrase of Numbers 6:24-26, followed by re-reading the story again of the little girl and her Daddy picking flowers. Let it all break into your soul. Then draw a picture in the space provided to remind you of this kind of admiration your Creator Father has for you.

Is your soul awakening?

LIFE TRANSFORMATION

"WAKAN TANKA (Great Mystery),
teach me how to trust my heart,
my mind, my intuition, my inner knowing,
the senses of my body, and the blessings of my spirit.
Teach me to trust these things so that I may enter
my Sacred Space and love beyond my fear,
and thus Walk in Balance
with the passing of each glorious Sun."

—Lakota Prayer

Have you ever been told, "Keep your personal life, work life, and spiritual life separate?" I remember the first time I heard that statement. It rubbed me so wrong. What about authenticity and transparency? How do you balance that with compartmentalization? Does not an authentic life stand in contrast to a compartmentalized life?

Early in my years of ministry, I was meeting regularly with a lady for discipleship and accountability. After months of weekly time together, she expressed the following words to me: *"I feel like you're perfect. It makes me feel depressed."* Wow! Those were some heavy words to hear.

What she was expressing is that she needed me to be willing to be transparent and authentic with her too. However, I was not engaging her in this way. In our times together, she shared many difficult struggles and battles. I focused on helping her see the Truth. I was reluctant to share my struggles and battles because I did not want to make myself look bad. I had an image to uphold —or so I thought. I could not tarnish that image. I also did not want to hear from her that my struggles and battles paled in comparison to hers.

For much of my life, I have wrestled with feeling not good enough or less than. I have always been labeled as being the "good girl" in the room because my dad or my husband was a pastor. Oh, if they only knew how I have screwed up royally before. I have also struggled with feeling like my battles were nothing compared to so and so. I was made to feel I was overreacting, and my feelings were not respected. Feeling trapped in a bubble of "you are too good to have issues", "your struggles are trivial" or "if they knew the real me, they would condemn and reject me" made being authentic and transparent very challenging.

It took time, but eventually, I had to face my fear of being transparent and authentic. I had to overcome my fear of opening-up and sharing more specifically and on a deeper level with her. While I felt like my battles must have seemed petty in her eyes, surprisingly, she did not make me feel like they were trivial in comparison.

I started trusting the process more that day and began to dismantle the lies of compartmentalization. This was the beginning of real-life transformation—the kind I had desired for so long but never experienced as a believer. Funny thing, this was the title of the accountability program we were using with our church at the time— "Life Transformation Groups" by Church Multiplication Associates. (Cole, n.d.)

Here is the thing about masking your feelings, you will lose your soul. Your whole being functions in response to the rest of your being. No system, organ, or function can work by itself. It is not possible. It is not how Creator intended you to live your life either. While sometimes we compartmentalize our lives for a short time to process all the feelings we may be experiencing, making a habit of keeping the boxes so tightly packed is quite harmful. God created us for relationships. We cannot isolate ourselves or our lives if we value the kind of relationships Creator intended for us.

When you live a life that is in neat and tidy boxes, you become great at avoiding others and/or masking your feelings. A co-worker is having a rough day. Avoiding the elephant in the room her recent discovery of her husband's affair and the impact that is having on her ability to perform at work, is expected. Instead of offering a word of encouragement or a safe place to land, avoiding the discussion is best, because that is not the time or place to discuss personal issues. After hours, your co-worker calls. Instead of answering, it's best to let it go to voicemail because discussing work-related matters or socializing with colleagues outside of the office is frowned upon. Sunday morning rolls along. Politely greeting your co-worker, and offering her a hug is a good thing to do. Expressing your sorrow for her struggles, mentioning you will be praying for her, and letting her know if she needs anything to just call seems to roll right off the tongue, though it is hardly heartfelt. She politely smiles and thanks you. Then turns away with a pit in her stomach.

Compartmentalization is a way of dissociating. It's easier to face the trials of our own lives when we block out the trials of other's lives. We go to work, focus, and get the job done. No time for building relationships. We go home, do our chores, run errands, and attend to the care of our family's needs. No time for quality time. We go to church, put in our time, pray, praise, and go home. No time to socialize, we have things to finish at home and to get ready for work the next day.

We tell ourselves we do not need friends—we do not have time to play. We do not need a vacation—that is for the weak. We do not do things we enjoy—because we just do not have time to get our never-ending "To Do List" done. So, we isolate and insulate our lives to stay focused, to protect our time, to set boundaries, but mostly to protect our hearts. Trauma hurts. Hurting people, hurt people. Walling off our lives and becoming completely unavailable to people keeps us from being hurt and from hurting others.

That co-worker? She tried to talk to you at work, after work, and then at church. However, you made no room in your protected life for Creator to work. He had allowed you to be the salve to someone else's hurting heart, and in so doing they would be the balm to your wounds too.

In time, you will no longer operate out of authenticity and an inner sense of guidance led by the Great Spirit. You will lose the satisfaction you gain by being the hands of Jesus to those who are hurting. You will lose the essence of what it means to be like Christ—a Christian. You will lose or never experience community and what it means to BE the Church.

You will lose what it means to love and be loved in return. In the end, you will lose your soul. You will be alive, but you will be dead on the inside.

Authenticity and transparency reveal the pain so the wounds can be cleaned, dressed, and healed. Authentic and transparent people go to work, focus on their job, but also take notice when someone is hurting. They come alongside and offer support, even though they too are hurting in other ways. They take the risk of vulnerability by showing their scars because they understand others may find comfort and hope from their experience.

Authentic and transparent people are selfless with their time. They are willing to stay up late watching a movie for the one-hundredth time with their kids because they will only be little for so long. They share their joys and their sorrows with their spouse and children. They teach their kids by sharing their mistakes and wins growing up.

Authentic and transparent people show up to be the Church, pray together, consider how to apply the teaching to their everyday life, cry out in praise—then, fellowship afterward with the Body as an important part OF the Body.

They volunteer to be the healing hands of Jesus to those in need throughout the week. They take the risk of living in community as The Church was instructed to do, practicing the one-another-ing found in the book of Acts.

Authentic and transparent people are willing to admit when they are wrong and say, "I'm sorry!" when they have caused hurt. Authentic and transparent people dare to admit fear, are honest when they feel down, and do not hide behind a curtain of superiority.

It takes courage and risk to be authentic and transparent. It takes wisdom from the Great Spirit within you to know when to speak and when to listen. Your willingness to be transparent will liberate you from a life of reckless abandon because you will truly be living a fully Spirit-led life.

With time, you will find your wounds healing, your passion for Creator growing, your compassion for others expanding, and blessings abounding. The Great Spirit will speak, and you will know and follow accordingly. You will learn that living an authentic and transparent life is utterly transforming.

"WAKAN TANKA (Great Mystery),
teach me how to trust my heart, my mind,
my intuition, my inner knowing,
the senses of my body, the blessings of my spirit.
Teach me to trust these things
so that I may enter my Sacred Space
and love beyond my fear,
and thus Walk in Balance
with the passing of each glorious Sun."

—Lakota Prayer

Questions to Ponder:

Do you live a masked or emotionally unavailable life?

If so, why? Have you ever thought about taking the mask off and opening-up?

Are you afraid of authenticity and transparency?

Do you see value in living an authentic and transparent life?

What risks do you see in living with more transparency?

What is one situation you are currently facing that could benefit from a more transparent approach?

What is one step you could take to be more authentic in your relationships?

How could you selflessly give of your time to serve the Body of Christ and be the hands of Jesus in your community?

Is your soul awakening?

DELAYED GRIEF

"When I think of death,
and of late the idea has come
with alarming frequency,
I seem at peace with the idea that
a day will dawn when I will no longer be
among those living in the valley of strong humors.
I can accept the idea of my own demise,
but I am unable to accept the death of anyone else.
I find it impossible to let a friend or relative go
into that country of no return.
Disbelief becomes my close companion,
and anger follows in its wake.
I answer the heroic question
"Death, where is thy sting?" with
"It is here in my heart and mind and memories."

—Maya Angelou

Have you ever lost someone or something that you held so dear, yet never really grieved? Maybe it was through the permanence of death or perhaps the lost love is still alive.

I recently learned of a colleague who had to labor for eight hours to deliver her stillborn baby. Just two days later she went back to work treating patients. A month later she was beginning to feel insurmountable grief. So, she asked for advice on how to manage grief while working with her pregnant patients.

The more I thought about her question, the more I agonized for her and others who jumped back to life as usual before having enough time to properly grieve a lost love. Oh, the sting! Facing your loss and truly allowing yourself the time to grieve is the best gift you can give to yourself and the best way to honor your loved one or that relationship.

Putting the loss away, never talking about it, or pretending everything is fine is the worst thing you could do. One day, your grief will come. It will blindside you like a tsunami of uncontrolled emotions and take you under its riptide. The recovery from grief at that point is much more painful and potentially more damaging than facing your grief at the time of loss.

Psychologists all agree the grieving process is different for everyone. On average it takes about two years to grieve a loss, whether at the time of loss or sometime later.

In my practice, walking people through grief is unavoidable. Their physical pain is often rooted in grief. Drawing attention to their grief is part of the healing process. If they refuse to consider how their grief is triggering their pain, they will heal very slowly or not at all. It is challenging to work with patients who refuse to see how their past emotional pain plays a powerful present-day role in their health.

You have probably said the statement _____ is a "pain in the neck" or "pain in the butt." That person or situation is causing you stress (aka grief) which your body is holding onto in your nervous system. Stored grief tends to hang out in the lower part of your neck, shoulders, hips, and/or lower back. There is speculation that women who suffer from frozen shoulder syndrome do so because of unresolved emotional pain. It is believed these unresolved emotions even have an impact on female hormones.

The nerves of the lower part of the cervical spine (neck) are closely related to the thyroid. Your thyroid in combination with the brain regulates your hormones. As the nerves leave the spine in the lower part of your neck, they travel across the shoulders and down the arms to your fingers. They pass through all the muscles of the arms. If you are experiencing chronic aches in a shoulder, hip, neck, or lower back, consider how current and stored emotions might be playing a role in your healing process.

Sorrow and grief are real. They are not signs of weakness or being dramatic. It is a deeply emotional and spiritual act to mourn.

For centuries cultures around the world have utilized rituals to support those in mourning. Native Americans perform tribal dances to mourn the loss of loved ones. Wailing Women in African cultures perform death wails as a keening or lament soon after the death of a loved one or a member of the tribe. These rituals help encourage grieving and purging of emotions. Living a life with pent-up pain will only lead to long-term suffering in physical, mental, or spiritual ways.

Carl Jung postulated that a soul battle is a spiritual problem, and a spiritual battle is a soul problem. Delayed grief is a soul battle and will often manifest itself as a spiritual problem. Take for instance someone who has been deeply wounded by a trusted loved one as a child. They probably had no idea they should grieve or even how to grieve. Later this pain can lead to that child questioning if there is even a God. Their soul pain is a spiritual problem. A person wrestling with soul pain will often be wrestling with physical, emotional, and/or spiritual problems. After all, a soul without the Giver of Peace experiences spiritual pain.

As you will recall, I had to face delayed grief (Pain, pg. 55). I was pulled out to sea and nearly drowned by the undertow of sorrow from childhood memories of that fateful day in Florida. It came out of nowhere. My heart was laid open and shattered like a little child whose toy had been smashed into pieces. I quickly and frantically picked up the broken parts of my heart that I had so carefully and lovingly wrapped in a blanket and stored away in the shadows of the walls thirty years prior. Humiliation, shame, and a completely broken heart were too much to bear any longer. It was safer to hide it away and move on. Years later, there I was, down on my knees like a little girl begging Creator Father to put all the shattered fragments back together again.

It took a long time to process and grieve. I had a life coach that I trusted with my life and knew she was a safe place to land. She walked alongside me and helped encourage me in my steps. Her support made the journey bearable.

I think we are afraid to grieve because we do not want to forget. Sometimes we are afraid to share with another person the special moments we shared with our loved one. The long weekend in the mountains with someone else might taint the memories we have with our loved one at the same place. Maybe we are just too afraid of the idea that "time will erase all memories," so we choose to hide our emotions. We might not remember every detail years from now, but we will not forget the memory.

Just because your grieving process ends, you may still find a wave of emotion wash over you. It may not take you under anymore, but you still notice the pull of the water as it recedes from the shore.

I still have quiet moments alone in my truck or while walking in the woods when the tide rises a little. I can let it out when I need to and keep on going.

Those formative years as a young girl changed me. I lost the one I held most dear. Ego was crucified. Self-confidence and passion for life were erased. My voice was stolen from me. I was told that the person I was created to be was not acceptable. So, the old Mindi, along with all her precious memories of love and ambition, was gently wrapped in a blanket and buried safely in the walls of my heart. This experience shaped the way I would live the rest of my life. I set out to become someone that everyone else wanted me to be.

While the pain of love and loss does not go away, the wounds heal, forgiveness has been given, and my soul has been restored; the beautiful memories I cherish will never fade. The sting is gone, but oh did it hurt until I was forced to grieve.

In 2022, for the first time in thirty years, I was able to sit at my farmhouse kitchen table in the Carolinas eating shrimp and grits with cocktail sauce for dipping. I cherished the memories of a time gone by, yet to my surprise I did not cry or wince that I was sharing that moment with someone else. I quietly smiled in my heart. I had not forgotten.

"Where, O death, is your victory? Where, O death, is your sting? ... But thanks be to God! He gives us the victory through our Lord Jesus Christ!" 1 Corinthians 15:55, 57

Questions to Ponder:

Who have you lost that you have not grieved? Is the person still living or have they passed?

Are you afraid to grieve? Why? What is holding you back from pouring out your anguish?

How is unresolved grief impacting your physical health?

How is unresolved grief impacting your spiritual health?

Do you see how a soul battle is a spiritual problem? Describe how this is playing out in your life.

Do you see how a spiritual battle is a soul problem? Describe how this is playing out in your life.

Is your soul awakening?

COURAGE

*"Time to pull up your courage.
This is going to hurt, but you'll be ok.
Jesus is with you. I promise"*

—Mama

There is nothing worse as a new mom than taking your baby to the hospital for a scheduled surgery, handing them over to the nurse, and then waiting for what feels like forever for them to be sent safely to recovery. The day I had to place my one-year-old in the hands of someone else to care for during one of the most painful and frightening moments of his little life still causes me agony. I remember whispering in his little ear with tears pouring down my cheeks, "Time to pull up your courage. This is going to hurt, but you'll be ok. Jesus is with you. I promise."

I will tell you what, those words were spoken to my soul as much as they were to his little heart. That was one of the most terrifying moments of my life. Except it was not paralyzing. I still mustered the courage to hand him over for that surgery.

Paralyzing fears are another thing. You know the kind… frozen stiff with fear. Please tell me I am not the only one with at least one paralyzing fear. You have one too, right? I mean, tell me you are afraid of tight roping across one-thousand-foot gorge with only a harness and a helmet to protect you? Maybe your fear is the idea of selling off everything you own to move across the globe to live in a remote village in Africa. Maybe your fear is an alligator mistaking you for food while taking a walk along the marshlands in a low country. Maybe your greatest fear is spiders.

For years, I used to have frightening dreams where I was unable to scream or move. Paralyzed and mute. No matter how hard I tried to scream for help or how hard I tried to pick up my feet to run, I was completely frozen. I never could understand why I was having such terrifying nightmares.

Several years ago, my life coach challenged me to conquer my greatest fears. At first, I thought, "Fears? I don't have any fears that are so big they need conquering." The more I thought about it over several days, I remembered I was utterly terrified of two things: heights and depths.

You might ask why I did not recall them right away. I think it was because I was in such a painful place in life. I had made a habit of avoiding everything that caused me to be uncomfortable, yet I was still miserable.

So, taking her advice, I set out to conquer my two greatest fears: heights and depths. Little did I know at the time, that these two fears were much bigger than they appeared on the surface. These fears were the undercurrent to my struggles as I would soon discover.

I realized I became terrified of anything having to do with height or depth as a young adult. However, I had no idea where these fears had come from. The older I got the more the fears grew to the point of feeling paralyzed at the very thought of standing near a window in a second-story building or not being able to go near the deep end of a pool. I had no physical trauma or near-death experiences that I could think of to cause me to be afraid, yet I had become utterly petrified. It was during these years, I had multiple nightmares where I was paralyzed in fear. Eventually, panic attacks, anxiety, and depression became a constant battle as well.

Years and years passed, yet the fear remained— festering, growing like a deep wound. Only now I was much older and mid-life changes began to sneak in. Before I knew it, I was in the middle of an existential crisis. Some would call it a mid-life crisis, but I must tell you, it was more like a whole-life crisis. I was forced to face some emotional wounds. I expected it to be a difficult journey. Yet, I was determined to fight to the other side to find peace. I often described how I felt like that of a caged songbird forced into captivity, having lost its voice. The desperation to escape was mounting. Like any caged animal, I was coming undone and losing my sanity. I had to find a way to escape and fast!

Along the journey, I spent many hours and days alone talking to Creator, basking in His Creation, and praying for answers. I prayed for it all to make sense. I wanted freedom from the turmoil, and release from the heartache and pain. I began to isolate myself and find ways to escape —avoidance, solitude, trips alone to the desert, the beach, the jetty, etc.

While I may have escaped the momentary stuff of my life, the Great Spirit never left me. I did not leave Him either. Joshua Tree National Park in California became my sanctuary and where Creator God showed himself to me in purely miraculous ways. I also made time to meet up with a few old friends. We talked, laughed, cried, and shared fond memories. These moments were salve to my wounded heart.

On this journey, without even realizing it, I conquered my fears! Without giving it a second thought, I had laughed with a dear friend in deep ocean waters up to my neck with the warm sunshine filling me with radiant joy. I chose to climb a one hundred forty-five-foot tower to its lookout deck—and leaned over the railing. Heights and Depths—on the same day! Later that night it hit me— without thinking about it, I had conquered my two greatest fears! I WON! I defeated heights and depths!

When I think back to those experiences, I realize my fear was not that of water or being too close to the edge. I was not afraid of dying. My intense fear was the growing need to face emotional pain that had never been addressed.

What I was afraid of, what caused me to become frozen with terror, was diving into the deep putrid waters of anguish, shame, and remorse, because facing those things would be agonizingly painful. No one wants to feel emotional pain like that twice. You could get sucked under and drown in the dangerous rip current of unrelenting pain.

I was also afraid of feeling uninhibited elation—pure joy like that of a child—because I was not good enough and not smart enough. I was ashamed. I was judged and condemned. I did not deserve to scale those heights or experience that kind of joy.

Just twenty-four hours before facing these fears, I was the passenger driving down a quiet highway with this same friend. As we drove, we sat in silence for what seemed like an hour. I remember feeling at peace, calm, serene—safe. It was as if whatever was happening at that moment was something you read about in books, but could never experience in real life. I remember the silence was broken by a familiar song we sang along to and laughed so hard we had tears rolling down our cheeks. Moments later another familiar song played, only this time we were silently shedding tears.

Did you catch what I said? I felt safe. SAFE! Safe enough to laugh and safe enough to cry. Safe enough to be silent and safe enough to express the fullness of emotion. I felt safe with my emotions and at peace in the moment.

I had never been able to do that before without hearing the voices from childhood telling me I was being dramatic and childish. I had never felt *safe* enough to express pure joy or grief. I had not felt *safe* enough to dive deep or soar high. It was *safer* to hold back, stuff it down and hide. Peace could only be experienced on the other side of the grave.

My greatest fears were present and ever-growing because I did not feel *safe*. It was because my friend made me feel *safe*, that I was able to conquer those fears.

I must say, it does not have to be grueling to face your fears. Change is easy, thinking about change is hard, remember? Thinking about our fears is so much harder than conquering them. While the act of conquering your fears may be challenging, I can assure you, that the mind games and voices in your head are far more agonizing.

Sometimes, you must look at a situation in your life and change the mental message you keep repeating. Instead of "I can't do it!", flip the message around when and say to yourself, "I DARE YOU to do it! I dare you to dig deeper. I dare you to climb higher. I dare you to scale and uncover all that is holding you back from being the incredible person God has created you to be. I dare you to experience the fullness of *life* He has gifted you here on earth. I *dare* you to find *peace*!

It was not too long ago my daughter was facing a challenge that brought with it many doubts and uncertainties. I remember telling her, "I dare you to do it." She replied, "What if I fail?" I replied, "What if you fly!"

Looking back, a lot has changed since that daring weekend. Each year has held growth beyond what I could ever imagine or dream. I have accomplished many things on my "Dream of Doing" list. I got my voice back. I can soar and I can go deep. I now allow myself to face slightly less terrifying fears and I continue to win! I do not have those paralyzing nightmares anymore. Instead, I have magical dreams that I am flying like a bird soaring high above the treetops and swooping down deep into the ocean and back up again. I am not afraid. I am SAFE!

If you recall from the Introduction, I am a watercolor artist. Recently, I entered one of my paintings into an art competition for a beautiful coffee table book celebrating fifty years of the arts in Johnston County, North Carolina. Now, I can boast, that I am an officially published watercolorist!

I was fearful about submitting my painting for that publication because I did not want to experience the fear of rejection. Never in my wildest dreams did I ever think I could paint, let alone create something worth publishing. Remember, I did not think I was good enough. Yet, I proposed in my heart to do it anyway. "No fear. I am good enough. If not for this publication, then for another. I won't quit until I win!" Sure enough, winner-winner chicken dinner! I was chosen as a spotlight artist in the publication.

Because I chose to conquer my greatest fears, a whole new world has opened to me. I am no longer afraid to try new things. I am good enough. I am no longer afraid of rejection. I deserve to win. I am no longer afraid to speak out and be authentic and transparent. I feel safe. I have peace. I am no longer afraid to *live*.

So how about you? Is it time to pull up your courage? It is going to hurt a little, but you will be ok. You will be more than ok. You will win. You are safe. I promise!

Questions to Ponder:

What are your greatest fears?

What is it you are afraid of?

What is at the root of that fear?

Are you willing to take a giant leap of faith to conquer that fear?

Imagine what it will feel like when you win.

Imagine what life will look like after you win.

What more can you do?

How much further can you push yourself to accomplish your dreams without fear?

Is your soul awakening?

PURGING

"...place it before God as an offering."

Romans 12:1-2 (MSG, 2018)

I spent several hours one beautiful spring Saturday in my rope hammock reading, daydreaming, praying, and being carried away to faraway lands on the wings of the breeze. It was beautiful, peaceful, and so relaxing gazing up at the clouds from under my pecan trees. During this time, my creativity and imagination were sparked. I came up with a new line of cards I wanted to paint. I designed in my mind some of the artwork I wanted to paint as well.

While there, the Spirit spoke to me, and my soul was pricked. It was time to clean out the old and make room for the new.

The act of cleaning out takes time. Decisions must be made about what to keep, what to toss, what to recycle, and what to donate. The mess I create accomplishing such a task is ridiculous! Once I start, I must finish it. I cannot stand to have the house turned upside down. Kind of like life. So, I took to my bedroom closet and dresser. It was time to start there. Ugh!

I had battled so much weight gain since Covid wreaked havoc on my brain. No matter how clean I ate, the battle raged. The desire to get back to a healthy weight was strong but daunting.

The most discouraging part about cleaning out clothes is trying to hold onto the ones that no longer fit with the hope they will one day grace my curves *again*. Therein lies the battle… the word *"again."*

The Spirit told me it was also time to change my mind about that too. Maybe the problem is not my diet. Maybe the problem is my mindset.

I love how The Message translation of the Bible paraphrases what Paul writes in Romans 12:1-2: *"So here's what I want you to do, God helping you: Take your everyday, ordinary life—your sleeping, eating, going-to-work, and walking-around life—and place it before God as an offering. Embracing what God does for you is the best thing you can do for him. Don't become so well-adjusted to your culture that you fit into it without even thinking. Instead, fix your attention on God. You'll be changed from the inside out. Readily recognize what he wants from you, and quickly respond to it. Unlike the culture around you, always dragging you down to its level of immaturity, God brings the best out of you, and develops well-formed maturity in you."* Romans 12:1-2 (Romans 12:1-2, MSG)

So that day, I laid down my weight at Creator God's feet as an offering. What that looks like is telling Creator, that it is no longer my battle. The battle is His. Every day, I must choose to surrender back over to Him. Sometimes, that means every moment of every day—every meal, every trip to the grocery store, every decision to eat or not eat something that looks delicious but is not good for me.

Placing my wants or desires on the sacrificial table gives Him back control of my weight. I can now embrace my curves while allowing the Great Spirit to help me make the best choices. It also means I can cease striving to look how the culture says I should. Trying to fit into cultural norms just brings me down and makes me feel so unlovely and unworthy. What a lie! Remember, from the chapter Sanctification (pg. 27), I am already perfect in His eyes.

Later that day, I went to my bedroom and began going through each drawer in my dresser. Then just like a huge pile of clothes teetering on collapse, my heart toppled over. Some of the clothes I was holding onto were still in my dresser because of the memories stitched into the hems.

At the same time, my playlist on the speakers conjured up feelings and emotions of another time and place. Just as soon as these songs ticked off on my playlist, I could feel the spirit of peace leaving me.

It was then I crumbled on top of that pile of clothing and cried for a minute. My heart broke *again* as I realized what I was still holding onto had nothing to do with my figure. Rather, those cracks and walls in my heart, at one time, held some of the most sacred memories of my life.

Creator has done a major reconstruction job over the last several years. My heart has been repaired, but the glue is still drying. This cleaning out of my closet is a reminder to me that sometimes the stuff I am holding onto is not for obvious reasons but rather deeper emotional reasons.

Taking the time to recognize those emotional bonds is the easy part. Deciding whether to hold onto or break those bonds is much harder. The actual decision is easy to make. Thinking about the decision is the hard part.

Read that *again*... Deciding is easy. Thinking about the decision is hard. Sound familiar?

I decided to toss those clothes—not into a bin to store in the shed for a day down the road when they might fit *again*. I can't wear them *again*. They would stir emotions from times past. <u>Peace is more important to me</u>.

Transforming my mind by changing the way I think... making room for the new. Now that is fun! Because let's face it. Since the pandemic, I have not bought many new clothes in the last couple of years—besides scrubs.

Questions to Ponder:

What are some things that you need to clean out to make room for the new?

Why are you holding onto these things?

Is today the day to unpack them and let them go?

Is your soul awakening?

CATHEDRALS

"He who refreshes others will himself be refreshed."

Proverbs 11:25

One of my favorite things I learned in my Fine Arts class in college was the awe-inspiring architectural feature of flying buttresses. These beauties are the weight-bearing arms of the dome or vaulted ceilings in many cathedrals around the globe. Their job is to hold up the dome by distributing all the weight and wind forced down through their arms into the ground.

While a critical structure, they also serve as glorious framing to the artwork inside the church. From the breathtaking paintings on the ceilings to the gilded gold leaf surfaces and beautifully carved wood ornamentals, these structures not only are incredibly functional, but they are also massively beautiful.

Many church architects of the 16th -18th centuries, realizing the strength of these structures, began to add more of them to the buildings so more glass windows could be installed to bring in more light to the otherwise dreary dark sanctuaries. Of course, this prompted artists to craft some of the most beautiful storytelling of all time with the leaded stained-glass depictions of Jesus, his Disciples, Mother Mary, and modern-day saints. Today these cathedrals are the highlight of many tourist stops throughout Europe and around the world.

When I lived in Germany, I visited several cathedrals and marveled at their magnificence. From the Ulm cathedral with the highest spire in the world to various smaller village churches along the way, flying buttresses were the primary stabilizing structure in these beautiful cathedrals.

Not long ago I visited a cathedral that was crafted in the French Gothic style here in America. It too had beautiful flying buttresses adorned with gilded gold leaf, surrounded by fantastic stained-glass windows. While there, I tried to soak it all in. Of course, I sensed in my soul the Spirit trying to speak to me, but I did not take the time to consider what He may be saying.

Occasionally, I flip back to the pictures I snapped and recall the beauty. A few years later, when one of those pictures popped up on my phone, I started to feel the Great Spirit speak to me again. So, I stopped to listen, and here's what He told me:

It takes a team of like-minded people to support me if I want to be successful. It does not matter what I do, I need a strong support system around me. These people need to be on the same page as me. They need to challenge me, yet still blow wind in my sails and have my back.

I need a few friends who will love me, comfort me, and hold me up when the storms of life come. I need friends who will not tear me down or let me crumble under the heavy weight of the struggle. They need to be strong and trustworthy, not weak.

The Spirit also caused me to ponder: Am I a flying buttress in the life of someone I care about? Am I a friend, a co-worker, or a family member who is strong trustworthy, steadfast, and not easily moved? Do I hold firm and bear the burden of another who needs my support and care during a time of pain, crisis, illness, or turmoil? Am I strong for them when they are weak?

My husband's mother passed away many years ago. She was a flying buttress in our life—a strong prayer warrior. We knew if we needed prayer, we could turn to her. She prayed for us daily and was always ready and waiting to pray specifically for our needs. When she passed, both my husband and I wondered, "Now who is going to pray for us?"

Over the years, God has brought several older women into my life who have become my flying buttresses. One of these cherished women I have known since I was a young girl. She has faithfully prayed for me over the years even when I was no longer living near her. Recently, I made a point of visiting with her while I was traveling. Upon seeing her, I was overcome with emotion and burst into tears. It was then I realized how important of a role she has played in my life for so many years. Creator God had answered my prayer of "who will pray for me?" by bringing Martha back into my life.

Whenever I have experienced a time when I am broken and weak, I cry out to God for help. He shows up and so do my flying buttresses in a way only they can be— strong & silent. In that moment, without knowing it, they lift me and carry my burden.

Questions to Ponder:

Who are your flying buttresses?

Who needs you to show up as their flying buttress?

How can you support them during their storm, lest they crumble under the weight?

Is your soul awakening?

SACRED DREAMING

"There is freedom waiting for you,
On the breezes of the sky,
And you ask, "What if I fall?"

Oh, but my darling,
What if you fly?"

—Erin Hanson

"A sacred dream launches you to a destiny beyond simply not dying, or of being reasonably happy as you strive to avoid discomfort. It encourages you to explore the mysteries of life and love, to glimpse a reality beyond death, and discover a timeless truth for yourself. It demands that you act boldly and courageously, and not collude with the consensual—that which everyone agrees on and no one questions—even though it is a popular story that traps us in daydreams that become nightmares. I discovered that when you hold a sacred dream, the universe begins to actively conspire on your behalf to make the impossible doable. Discovering the sacred dream requires courage. You can no longer be a passive (and anxious) bystander watching others have a meaningful life. The sacred dream will not come knocking at your door: It requires that you leave the familiar and embark on a quest. It requires that you not compromise your integrity. It demands that you not allow yourself to be seduced by the "easy path." It calls you to fight the lie that your daydream is adequate and will continue to keep you comfortable. This is why it is called the way of the luminous warrior." Alberto Villoldo (Villoldo, 2009)

…the way of the luminous warrior… Whew!

When I began the outline for writing this book, I remembered this paragraph from when I read *Courageous Dreaming* several years ago. So, I quickly added it to my list of concepts to cover so I would not forget to include it.

Going through my notes, as I embarked to write this chapter, I re-read those words describing the luminous warrior. I was taken aback all over again. There is something so noble, strong, and powerful in Villoldo's literary description of such a warrior. I would like to parse out this excerpt a little because I believe it has serious implications for how we think, what we believe, and how we live our lives every day. To me, the luminous warrior is someone who is full of Light and embraces the Power and Strength from within —the Creator's God-breathedness. This luminous warrior shines Light into the dark places and fights for Truth. The luminous warrior is full of courage and must embark on the quest to live a life free from the status quo. The luminous warrior sees the bigger picture and is willing to tread the road less traveled to live their sacred dream.

The American people enjoy a very comfortable life. No matter how rich or poor you may be in this country, you live a far more comfortable existence than much of the rest of the world. Most of us will never really know what it means to go without our basic needs being met for even a day. We work hard, get paid, and for the most part, enjoy a plentiful life. Yet we put up boundaries or barriers to keep harm away and protect us from pain.

Why? So, we can live safely? So we don't get hurt? No! So, we cannot die! That is the real reason we protect ourselves, is it not? No one likes discomfort. Everyone wants to be happy. No one wants to be hurt or to die.

But wait... what about living? Do you erect walls around your life to keep people out or to keep yourself in? Do you feel you do not deserve to experience pleasure in life? Do you feel guilty when you achieve success, therefore it is safer for you to insulate and isolate.

If you are destined to follow the way of the luminous warrior, you must free yourself to dream sacred dreams. In other words, you must set aside your fears, so you can allow your imagination to take flight. Sacred dreams are bigger than a goal or vision. They are the imaginings of explorations to experience life and love, glimpses of reality and life beyond death, and discovering timeless truths.

Do you recall how I discussed how our actions and mindset today affect our descendants generations from now? Imagine with me how your dreams and visions today are shaping the future world in which your children and children's children will live.

Our 5x great-grandparents envisioned and created the world we experience today. They did so by their intentions and actions 150 years ago. Your current attitude and outlook on life, the world you create around you today, and the future you imagine shape the world of tomorrow.

Even the Bible is clear about how our actions impact our children and beyond. Not only are the sins of the father passed down for generations, but so are the dreams and good deeds, values and morals, faith and honor, and more importantly Creator's blessings! You can find countless references throughout all of Scripture if you would like to study this more.

The precursor to sacred dreaming requires you to be bold and courageous. *"Haven't I commanded you? Be strong and courageous, don't be afraid or dismayed, for the Lord your God is with you everywhere you go"* Joshua 1:9.

You cannot dream of the future and imagine it into existence if you do not dare to let go of your fears and trauma. You cannot be bold if you are holding onto old wounds. Fear and trauma do not serve you. They enslave you. You must be bold and courageous if you are to dream sacred dreams, remembering that the Great Spirit is with you everywhere you go! Why then do you live in fear of dying or living?

To live the way of the luminous warrior, you must not live the consensual life. Accepting tradition without questioning its origin, intention or accuracy does not create luminosity. Rather, it creates compliance or consent. When you measure everything against the truth, you begin to illuminate the faulty ideology or notion that consensual life is always right. Yet, it is certainly the easier path—the one of least resistance. The unexamined life is the consensual life. It is the agreed upon unquestioned popular story that traps us in a daydream that becomes a nightmare.

Let me give you an example. The consensual life of the average American says we are to rise early, eat a good breakfast, work hard all day, eat a good dinner, and then go to bed early. We should avoid all forms of dissension, live an ethical life, be positive, and do good. We are to do our duty as citizens of the United States by voting for the popular candidate, speaking against those whom we disagree with, fighting for our liberty and freedom, and paying our taxes.

If you are a Christian, it also means reading your Bible and praying every day, accepting whatever is preached from the pulpit as truth without consideration, and being obedient without questioning authority. Agree that drinking, drugs, and sex outside of marriage are sins. Acknowledge that the Ten Commandments are not suggestions. Dress modestly and without excess, as a sign of humility and morality.

While some of these things you would likely believe are acceptable, some of these probably prick your skin and ruffle your feathers. I would imagine if you have made it to this final chapter, some of what I have said you agree with, while some has certainly raised your eyebrows a few times and caused you to bristle against what I wrote.

What if your sacred dream looked something like this:

Every morning, rising together with the sun and all of creation, you wrap yourself in a soft blanket to sit in silence while observing and listening to nature as it awakens and blossoms. All the while, sipping your morning coffee or tea while reclining on your porch rocking chair, breathing deeply, and meditating on a chosen word, Scripture, song, or idea.

With your eyes closed, you begin to envision images that reflect your meditative thoughts. These images begin to take on color, personality, and life. Perhaps they are images of a time gone by or perhaps they are images of a future time and place. These images begin to take on a deeper meaning and stir emotion within you. Perhaps they call you to action. Maybe they call you to rest. A sacred dream always calls you to boldness and courage.

Sacred dreaming is like opening a special gift box. Slip the ribbon off. Carefully peel back the tape. Now, gently pull the gift wrap away from the box. With great intention and magical anticipation, slowly open the lid. Can you see the treasure inside? What is it you see?

This is the point… I did not choose to reveal all I have written in the pages of this book, nor asked you to contemplate the principles herein to make you feel good. I seek to help you open your eyes to more—far more than you can imagine! I choose to show you a way of being, thinking, and living that can only happen when you decide to release your trauma and fear. You decide the timing.

The Great Spirit is calling you to something far bigger and grander than the existence you currently live—an existence that is so sacred and so daring it will change the course of your life and that of generations to come! You can choose to go your merry way and continue to ignore the pricking and prodding of the Spirit, or you can stop mindlessly following the "way it is" or "the way it has always been"—the consensual life—and begin to discover the *abundant* life that is waiting for you!

Barriers, isolation, insulation, unresolved grief, buried trauma, and even some religious practices and ideals are erected to insulate and protect your heart, mind, soul, or physical body from the possibility of death—or truly living. While they may help you to live a safe and comfortable life you are just dying—a soul death. They serve as a gilded enclosure adorned with crystals and a glistening gate, pretty music, a swing, daily clean water, and fresh food. The enclosure keeps you from harm and protects you from evil. Your needs are met—fresh air, clean water, and food. Yet you soon discover what seems like the perfect daydream is a nightmare—like a songbird locked in a cage.

You may not see anything wrong with this. I mean, birds make wonderful pets. They sing, talk to you, are sweet company, and are easy to get along with. Many people have pet birds, and they all seem to live happily in their cages.

It is nice to observe wild birds living a carefree life as they fly up to the window next to your cage, perch on the sill, sing, and chatter with you through the glass; only to fly off again to wherever the wind takes them. After all, you are civilized, cultured, well-groomed; sheltered from the storms, hot sun, parched, and dry land. They, on the other hand, are wild and prey to the beasts of the field. You do not have to search for food, peck from the ground, or keep an eye out for predators. You enjoy a certain pedigree. You are comfortable, warm, safe, and secure inside. They, however, are... free.

This caged existence is not the way of the luminous warrior. To follow the way of the luminous warrior, you can no longer be a passive and anxious bystander watching the free birds around you have an abundant and meaningful life while you stay safely locked in a dark, dimly lit cage protected from harm.

However, the cage door will not be opened for you. The only way of escape is to break the gate open. You must leave the familiar and comfortable surroundings and embark on a quest to experience true freedom. This freedom does not mean you will compromise your integrity, but it does mean you might have to discard some of the safeguards that have been erected that only serve to enslave you.

The way of the luminous warrior will lead you down some challenging roads. Do not be seduced to take the easy path. The easy path is to return to the familiar and safe existence inside the cage—the institution, the religious traditions that are not biblical but rather cultural, the protected life with all its barriers and cushions to insulate.

These constructs are a lie and will not keep you safe and comfortable. They are not adequate. They enslave. They are dangerous. They are life-sucking, not life-giving. They are dark and cold.

Don't get me wrong. I am not saying there is no truth in these constructs. I am asking you to consider the ideals that are not full of Light from The Great Spirit.

"Be careful that no one captivates you with philosophy and empty deception from their human tradition that is based on world principles and not from the teachings of Christ" Colossians 2:8.

How many lifestyle and faith traditions have you accepted as true &/or Biblical that are purely cultural? Likewise, how many cultural traditions have you been denied because they have been considered "unbiblical?" Seriously, think about that.

A native tribal leader and pastor of an indigenous evangelical church recently discussed with me the importance of accepting your identity and embracing an authentic life that honors Creator God in all aspects of life, including worshiping the Creator. He urged me to consider how evangelical Christian tradition has condemned dancing, drums, rattles, incense, feathers, and the like. They were stripped from the Native American cultural practice of Christian worship many years ago when colonists took their Sacred Land. Colonists believed the Indigenous symbols were demonic and had no place in a Christian's life, let alone the church. So, when they began to evangelize the native tribes while simultaneously stealing their Sacred Land hundreds of years ago, they stripped them of all that was sacred and culturally native. The natives refer to this as "whitewashing."

However, this washing away to make them appear "godly" was not of God. It was the Apostle Paul who said,

"I have become all things to all people so that by all possible means I might save some" I Corinthians 1:22b.

Native Americans have long used instruments and natural elements in their worship of Creator God. Simply because the colonists could not understand their language and identify with their culture, they feared what they could not understand. Their fear and insatiable greed changed the sacred dream inspired by Creator God of the Native American world when their Sacred Land was destroyed, and their spiritual and cultural practices were demonized.

Despite all this, there are a few luminous warriors who broke free from their cages and illuminated a path to the sacred dream. Today, there are Christian churches in tribes all around the country that are beginning to reclaim their cultural practices and traditions in the worship of Creator by writing new music in their native tongue accompanied by drums, rattles, and singers. These worship songs are sung in the same fashion as songs played during powwows.

Dancers are encouraged to dance before the Lord adorned in their beautiful regalia with their feathers, hoops, ribbons, scarves, and jingles. It is not chaotic and disorderly. It is quite beautiful and orderly.

The leader's teaching is like that of an elder sharing oral tradition while reading from the Bible. Multiple generations of Christians worship together in a sacred circle. They fellowship together, practicing the gift of hospitality. They welcome new people into their circle with glad and sincere hearts.

Their spiritual gatherings reflect their cultural identity. They look and sound like an indigenous church, not a

Euro-centric church. These churches are reshaping and changing the future of what it means to be a Native American Christian not only for their generation today but for many generations to come.

This sacred dream has taken enormous courage for the native people. They have faced unrelenting resistance from traditional evangelical Christians both inside the native community and from outside. Some leaders have lost everything in their pursuit to break free of the cage that enslaved them. However, they continue to press on, because they know that the way of the luminous warrior requires courage, authenticity, cultural and spiritual integrity, a willingness to take the path less traveled—and to somehow regain their Sacred Land in honor and worship of Creator God.

To choose to follow Jesus alone, the perfect Luminous Warrior, to take risks without fear of failure, to be authentic to yourself and others around you, to be transparent as an open book, to truly love others as Jesus loves them, to SOAR in freedom, to question tradition and status quo, to discern what is taught vs. blindly believe, to live a reality beyond death—of life Eternal, to discover timeless Truths for yourself, to dispel fear in and darkness around you with the Light of Christ and all His Power ALIVE in you—this is the way of the luminous warrior.

What if I fall?
But, oh my darling, what if you fly?

Questions to Ponder:

STEP 1:
On a sheet of paper, draw a bird cage with a bird inside. Make it a colorful drawing even if it's chicken scratch. Inside the cage, write your name on the bird, and write all the things in life that keep you "safe." On the outside of the cage, write all the things that you "need" protected from.

STEP 2:
Now make a list of what it would look like if you could break free from the "cage."

STEP 3:
Only when you are good and ready... full of boldness and courage, strength, faith, trust, and no fear... tear that piece of paper into a million little pieces the size of dimes or smaller. With each rip, declare your freedom, dispel the fear, dispel the darkness, dispel the lies, dispel the status quo, dispel the cultural and religious traditions, and dispel the chains that enslave you.

STEP 4:
Gather all the tiny pieces of paper into your hands. Do not miss a single piece. Now, take a huge deep slow breath in, to the count of three, hold for the count of three, then toss the pieces into the air above your head as you exhale with a loud burst, screaming the words I AM FREE!

Now, how did you feel drawing the bird in the cage as a depiction of yourself and your current state?

How did you feel when you were listing all the safety measures you have employed to keep you safe?

How did you feel when you were listing all the things you were protecting yourself from?

How did you feel when you were tearing up the paper, dispelling all the crud?

How did you feel when you took that deep breath in, held it, and then exploded by throwing those pieces high into the air while screaming as you set yourself free?

Now how do you feel?

Is your soul awake?

Have you broken free?

SINGING I GO...

"She laid there
in the morning light.
I took shelter upon her breast
close to her heart
and listened.
Behind her rib cage
was the meaning to life.
There was a songbird
ready to take flight."

—Author Unknown

Beautiful songbird, I applaud you for your courage and strength to break free from your cage. I applaud you for your bravery to face your pain, work through it, and begin the journey toward peace. I encourage you to read this book time and again, stopping to process through the questions and activities. They are designed to help you contemplate and envision a life of peace.

As you work through these chapters over and again, be reminded, that I do not claim to be a mental health expert and my writings are not intended to replace the role of a professional therapist. Should you find yourself struggling with emotional health, please seek professional help.

As you have discovered, this book helped you to identify your pain. Hopefully, you were able to identify the *root* of your pain. This is the first step towards peace.

My next book, "Pain to Peace: Rise Up and Soar," will help you grow in your newfound freedom, find the strength to fly, and guide you towards experiencing wondrous moments with the Spirit.

Remember, this is a journey not a quick weekend getaway. So go back and take your time wrestling through each chapter. The Spirit will continue to reveal what He wants you to discover if you give room for and follow His promptings.

As part of your journey, in addition to speaking engagements and wellness events, I host Pain to Peace wellness events around the country to help other women like you (sorry men) move from pain to peace.

I invite you to join me for a rejuvenating day or weekend of wellness. It's time to bid farewell to pain and embrace peace! During these wellness events, you will discover a wide array of activities designed to help you achieve optimal well-being. From prayer and meditation sessions to holistic healing and mindfulness practices, these events offer something for everyone.

Learn about herbal remedies and essential oils that can soothe your body and mind. Immerse yourself in the serene surroundings of Creation as you participate in guided nature walks and a sound bath or stretching session. Feel the stress melt away as you connect with the healing power of nature and its Creator.

Join me, as I share valuable insights on stress management, nutrition, and self-care. Gain practical tips and tricks to incorporate wellness into your daily life.

As a fellow songbird on this journey, don't miss the opportunity to embark on a guided experience from pain to peace. Visit Black Eyed Susan Media's website for more information on hosting and/or attending a Pain To Peace Wellness Day in your community. Isn't it time to spread your wings and fly towards a healthier, happier you?

PSALM 139

For the director of music. Of David. A psalm.

You have searched me, Lord,
and you know me.
You know when I sit and when I rise;
you perceive my thoughts from afar.
You discern my going out and my lying down;
you are familiar with all my ways.
Before a word is on my tongue
you, Lord, know it completely.
You hem me in behind and before,
and you lay your hand upon me.
Such knowledge is too wonderful for me,
too lofty for me to attain.

Where can I go from your Spirit?
Where can I flee from your presence?
If I go up to the heavens, you are there;
if I make my bed in the depths, you are there.
If I rise on the wings of the dawn,
if I settle on the far side of the sea,
even there your hand will guide me,
your right hand will hold me fast.
If I say, "Surely the darkness will hide me
and the light become night around me,"
even the darkness will not be dark to you;
the night will shine like the day,
for darkness is as light to you.

For you created my inmost being;
you knit me together in my mother's womb.
I praise you because I am fearfully and wonderfully made;
your works are wonderful,
I know that full well.
My frame was not hidden from you
when I was made in the secret place,
when I was woven together in the depths of the earth.
Your eyes saw my unformed body;
all the days ordained for me were written in your book
before one of them came to be.
How precious to me are your thoughts, oh God!
How vast is the sum of them!
Were I to count them,
they would outnumber the grains of sand —
when I awake, I am still with you.

If only you, God, would slay the wicked!
Away from me, you who are bloodthirsty!
They speak of you with evil intent;
your adversaries misuse your name.
Do I not hate those who hate you, Lord,
and abhor those who are in rebellion against you?
I have nothing but hatred for them;
I count them my enemies.
Search me, God, and know my heart;
test me and know my anxious thoughts.
See if there is any offensive way in me,
and lead me in the way everlasting.

Lakota Prayer

Oh, Great Spirit,
whose voice I hear in the winds
and whose breath gives life to all the world, hear me.
I am small and weak.
I need your strength and wisdom.
Let me walk in beauty and make my eyes
ever behold the red and purple sunset.
Make my hands respect the things you have made
and my ears sharp to hear your voice.
Make me wise so that I may understand
the things you have taught my people.
Let me learn the lessons you have hidden
in every leaf and rock.
I seek strength, not to be superior to my brother,
but to fight my greatest enemy - myself.
Make me always ready to come to you
with clean hands and straight eyes,
so when life fades, as the fading sunset,
my spirit will come to you
without shame.

~Lakota Indian Chief Yellow Lark – 1887

ACKNOWLEDGMENTS

The Great Spirit, Creator God—the Author of my life.

Katja Jentes Bruton—your relentless design skills blow me away.

Kayla Jentes-Sagester—for gently walking this journey with me for so many years and putting the final edits on this book.

Bev Gillespie—the world's greatest proofreader and an even better friend.

Maria Brown—a sweet spirit who gently guided me and shared her wisdom as a beta reader for my manuscript.

Mike Jentes—we're halfway there—living on a prayer.

Dad—for always being there to gently guide me through the waters of life.

Mom—for teaching me just about everything I know to survive this crazy life.

WORKS CITED

Cole, N. (n.d.). *Starling Initiatives*. Retrieved from www.starlinginitiatives.com: https:// directionjournal.org/38/2/intertext-messaging-e c h o e s - o f - aaronic.html#:~:text=The%20Lord%20make%20his %20face%20shine%20upon%20you%20and%20be,b e%20placed%20over%20the%20people

English Standard Version. (2001-2004 Crossway). Retrieved from www.esv.org: https://www.esv.org/ resources/esv-global-study-bible/introduction-to-jonah

Martens, E. (Fall 2009; Vol.38. No.2.). *Direction Journal*. Retrieved from www.DirectionJournal.org: https:// directionjournal.org/38/2/intertext-messaging-e c h o e s - o f - aaronic.html#:~:text=The%20Lord%20make%20his %20face%20shine%20upon%20you%20and%20be,b e%20placed%20over%20the%20people

The Message Bible. (2024, Bible Study Tools). Retrieved from www.biblestudytools.com: https:// www.biblestudytools.com/msg/romans/ passage/?q=romans+12:1-2

Muka T, K. F. (2016;212:174-83). The role of epigenetic modifications in cardiovascular disease: a systemic review. *Int J Cariol*.

Ventana Wildlife Society. (n.d.). Retrieved from www.ventanaws.org: https://www.ventanaws.org/condors.html? gclid=CjwKCAiA85efBhBbEiwAD7oLQNsPKontQ uqo1QUB2GPI971wV9YJW79ol8YDfLJSMZN9deY nPL1ngRoCz2kQAvD_BwE

Villoldo, A. (2009). *Courageous Dreaming*. Hay House.

ABOUT THE AUTHOR

Dr. Mindi Miller-Jentes is a board-certified chiropractic physician in North Carolina, author, watercolorist, and speaker. She helps audiences nationwide to understand the importance of overcoming negative self-talk and destructive emotions. Dr. Miller-Jentes is a national and international  resource on the body-mind-spirit connection and the role this connection plays in physical and emotional health. She shares information about supporting a healthy lifestyle at www.BrioWellness.com. Dr. Miller-Jentes is the CEO and co-owner of Brio Wellness Center - a holistic, family-operated chiropractic clinic in North Carolina where she lives with her husband. Her mission is to help everyone to live the life they desire and deserve.

Facebook.com/mindimillerjentes

Instagram.com/mindimillerjentes

SHARE YOUR THOUGHTS

With the author: Your comments will be forwarded to the author when you send them to info@blackeyedsusanmedia.com.

With Black Eyed Susan Media: Submit your review of this book by writing to info@blackeyedsusanmedia.com.

Visit Our Website:

www.BlackEyedSusanMedia.com

https://facebook.com/BlackEyedSusanMediaLLC

https://instagram.com/blackeyedsusanmedia/

A BLACK EYED SUSAN MEDIA PUBLICATION

COMING SOON
BY MINDI MILLER-JENTES, DC

Summer 2024:
Con Brio! In the Kitchen with Dr. Mindi
in collaboration with Brio Wellness Center

Spring 2025:
Pain to Peace: Rise Up & Soar